WHEN THE
NIGHT IS
TOO LONG

WHEN THE
NIGHT IS
TOO LONG

Robert L. Wise

THOMAS NELSON PUBLISHERS
Nashville

Copyright © 1990 by Robert L. Wise

Published in Nashville, Tennessee, by Thomas Nelson, Inc., and distributed in Canada by Lawson Falle, Ltd., Cambridge, Ontario.

Printed in the United States of America.

Scripture quotations are from the REVISED STANDARD VERSION of the Bible. Copyright © 1946, 1952, 1971, 1973 by the Division of Christian Education of the National Council of the Churches of Christ in the U.S.A. Used by permission.

Epigraphs at the beginning of each chapter are the author's own translation.

Library of Congress Cataloging-in-Publication Data

Wise, Robert L.
    When the night is too long / Robert L. Wise.
      p.   cm.
    Includes bibliographical references.
    ISBN 0-8407-7159-2
    1. Consolation. 2. Suffering—Religious aspects—Christianity.
3. Wise, Robert L. I. Title.
BV4905.W58 1990
248.8'6—dc20   89–48777
                                             CIP

To my children and grandchildren
who have made so much hope possible
during all of the difficult times:
Todd, Tony, Tate, Traci,
Rachael, Zac, and Tabitha.

CONTENTS

Acknowledgments

These pages are the product of the struggle of living through hard times, assisted by people who have been my gracious, kind, and loving friends. Without their listening, thoughtful responses, it would not have been possible. I'm particularly indebted to my friends Dale Assink, Mac McAbee, Diana Waters, Joanna Smith, Larry Jones, and Betty Mansfield for the hours they've spent listening. As always, I am in debt to Jeannie Rogers, my administrative assistant, for her counsel, secretarial skills, and gracious, unending help in preparing this manuscript for publication.

The stories within these pages are all true accounts. With the exception of one request for privacy, all are the actual names and identities of people who have courageously shared their pain. For their willingness to be vulnerable for the sake of giving hope to others, I deeply thank them.

"Because Pain Is a Condition of Human Existence, It Cannot Be Removed Once and for All."

K. C. Joseph Jurismmotil
Heaven & Hell on Earth:
An Appreciation of Five
Novels of Graham Greene

Weeping may tarry for the night,
but joy comes with the morning.
Psalm 30:5b

WHEN THE
NIGHT IS
TOO LONG

PREFACE

As a pastor, counselor, and friend I have had the privilege of trying to help others make sense out of questions, experiences, and feelings that suggest there is no real justice in this world, no lasting love in relationships, and just maybe no God in the heavens. Such times produce their own logic of despair which melts rationality away, leaving us feeling hopelessly deceived. In such a dark night of the soul, I know how important it is to find a light.

A decade ago, I wrote *When There Is No Miracle*, which explored the problem of pain. The book prompted many letters which helped me find a new dimension to the problem of innocent suffering. I discovered that as people deal redemptively with tragedy, something important happens. They recover their souls. A renewed spiritual vitality changes how they relate to others, to themselves, and finally to their pain. Something much bigger than an answer is recovered. New meaning and purpose in life arise from the depths of their being. Therefore, I am writing again to explore further how pain can help us to find our souls.

Frequently writers address the problem of suffering as if lofty, academic answers could alleviate personal tragedy. Such comforters are descendants of the friends of Job. Their approach offends most of us intellectually and emotionally. However, for a moment, let's consider the scholarly, objective approach to illuminating the dark night with bright ideas.

Suffering is far too personal ever to be treated as a classroom subject for which somewhere there is a right answer. Creation itself is so constructed that it generally will not cough up the rhyme and reason that make broken dreams and promises whole again. If one sallies forth seeking vindication by finding out the reason for innocent suffering, no satisfactory answers will be found. The world doesn't yield emotionally satisfying, abstract answers for this quest. Generally all we get back are more questions that only help reframe our original inquiries so that better questions are asked. Eventually we get down to a few right questions that help us see into the ultimate nature of reality; but that's about the best that we do.

My second son, Tony, is a writer and college instructor. Recently he observed that he went to the university expecting to find a depository where all the answers are kept. Tony finds that his students come with the same idea. However, time has taught him that perspective is unproductive and won't yield much of an education. Now Tony views college as a place of questioning where the goal is not to find answers but to learn to ask the right questions. I find his insight profound. So it is with the problem of pain. Courage to carry on is far more important than what we think we know.

Occasionally people want answers that can be used like pacifiers. Hoping to be able to suck on an explanation hard enough, they can ignore the rest of the problem—and the world. Solutions to the agonizing issues of desolation are never intended to be of that order. Pain has a priceless potential to open hearts and souls to a depth of sensitivity that is recovered through nothing save hard times. Our need is not so much to shut off the mind's quandary as it is to open the heart's doors. That which we cannot understand may force us to become what otherwise we could never have been. Often midnight wrestling matches with invisible angels of God are the only encounters which can open our eyes to the realities of a world overflowing with visible need and in want of human kindness. Therein do we recover our souls.

Suffering has the potential to break the molds into which we have poured all of our experiences. When the lens through which we see the world gets shattered by hard knocks and bumps, new and more profound perceptions appear. Such realizations are not possible apart from those turbulent times that knock us to the ground.

And where is God in all of the confusion? My experience has been that most often absence is one of the ways He chooses to be present. Hiddenness seems to be one of His unique strategies. He uses the night like a craftsman wields his finest tool. So the absence of light is an invitation to us to keep on searching for where He has stored the candles.

Christian tradition asserts that Jesus Christ was born at midnight because it is darkest then—and that is the time He is most needed. So let's push on through the night, looking for lamps, handholds, bridges, ladders, and a few matches that He has given to us. Even in the darkest of times, I think we will discover that God is still working for good.

Robert L. Wise
24 December 1988
Oklahoma City, Oklahoma

PART ONE

*When
All
the Lights
Have
Gone Out*

*DOES
GOD
WORK
IN
ANYTHING
FOR
WHATEVER?*

1

HAS GOD ABANDONED ME OR DID I ABANDON HIM?

The night has often been too long for me.

On many occasions the hours have been unbearable.

I remember when the shadows and murkiness began. Even though I was no more than four years old, the memory is vivid and indelible. The experience repeated itself over countless nights. Only as an adult was I sure the recollection was really merely a dream and not a flashback. Yet it came over and over filling my dark room with emotions that lingered long after images had faded.

Like an old movie seen again and again, the scene always opened with my playing between rows of cotton plants that grew higher than my head. Scurrying between the rows, I peeked out and discovered workers were being loaded up at the end of the field. My mother was climbing into the back of the truck with other people. Instantly, I knew I would be left. Running as fast as my little legs would carry me, I darted desperately through the plants trying to catch the truck; but the roar of the motor drowned out my cries and the old wreck went bouncing off down the road. Once it turned the bend, it disappeared behind huge cottonwood trees. With dust flying, I was left standing in the field as night fell.

Often I woke up apprehensively staring into the night because the darkness seemed so impenetrable and the emptiness so vast and foreboding. As an adult, my dreams changed, but the nature of the darkness never did. My journey and the need for consolation began there.

Through the passing years, others have told me countless stories of how their own visitations of pain seemed
to come with greatest urgency just after eyelids had
closed and their minds appeared to have shut up shop on
the assaults of the day. Generally somewhere between
two and three o'clock, the plug seems to be pulled on all
of the earthquake feelings that have been kicked downstairs in hope that after-shocks will never have to be
measured. Those times of tremor are seasons when the
night becomes too long.

FROM OUT OF THE DARKNESS

The passing of decades has brought me face to face
with what was boiling up in the middle of the night. Only
after years of excruciating times of darkness did I begin
to understand. As we talk about your struggles with suffering, I want to tell you about mine because beneath the
debris of yesterday, I found my soul. I believe you can
too.

The universe is filled with people who have experienced more physical, emotional, and mental pain than
either you or I will ever know. And yet, that doesn't diminish our own suffering. Whether it is more painful to
lose two legs or to sever an entire arm is a moot point if I
have just lost my hand. No one need apologize for how
their suffering finishes in some national pain contest.
Our concern is for getting on with the only life we have
to live. With that context in mind, I want to reveal my
soul to you as we ponder the difficult experiences life has
given us.

But first let me tell you about the experiences of some
of my friends.

After one dark night, June found herself confronted
with the same question I had faced so many years ago.
Have I been abandoned?

June had been married for twelve years when her
marriage began to crumble. She struggled and tried but
after a four-month separation, the inconceivable came.
June felt as if she would disintegrate under the weight of

failure. Thoughts of suicide flooded her mind and only one obstacle stood in her way: Heather, her beautiful six-year-old daughter.

Heather had always been a source of joy to June but divorce had devastated both of them. The child began manifesting dramatic symptoms signaling a desperate need for reassurance that she would not be abandoned. June promised Heather she would never leave her, and she knew she could never go back on that vow.

The final divorce was granted on a bleak Thursday afternoon, and June's depression turned into despair. The following Wednesday, as she drove alone in her car, tears suddenly came in such a flood she could barely see. But at the same moment, warmth seemed to arise from within and she felt as if from somewhere a Divine voice was saying, "I love you." Profound self-acceptance flooded her mind and brought a sense of reassurance so awesome that she found it nearly impossible to grasp what was happening.

However, when June got home that day, she discovered Heather was running a fever. June immediately took her to the doctor. The diagnosis was Reyes Syndrome. On Friday afternoon, Heather died.

Within eight days, June had lost her marriage and her only child. Night became like a shroud on a planet that seemed to be spinning into an endless blackness of empty space. June had discovered a level of pain beneath despair.

Is there any sense to be made of this story of June and Heather? At the end of this chapter I will tell you something of what unfolded in subsequent years, but for now we have a good case study in pain. The fact that the world is filled with many such stories may mean nothing. But if just one of these tales is our own, we are compelled to look anywhere for any hope we can find.

Like June, our plight can also become desperate. And if no clues are found, we must end up with Sartre, Camus, and Heiddeger in their conclusion that life is absurd. Sartre's *Nausea* aptly describes how such thoughts make us feel. Surely the philosophies of this world have only magnified the inconsistencies in human experience. I conclude that our questions are so imponderable that it is no cop-out to turn to people who feel they have insight from beyond this world. We need the loftiest perspective that can be found. Therefore, listening to voices that try to describe a sound heard from on high is appropriate.

FINDING A GUIDE

I find in the life of a little Jewish man named Saul of Tarsus an amazing amount of insight into this problem. While our birthdates made it impossible to meet, I have studied his writings so deeply that I consider him to be a good personal friend. What I can best reconstruct of his life indicates that for a period of time bitterness had completely swallowed his rationality. When Saul encountered people who had religious ideas different from his own, he could become so angry he would even try to kill them. Vilifying reputations and spreading dissension seems to have become something of an art with him. Although he was fundamentally a religious man, during this period of his life he exhibited the worst possible emotional and spiritual qualities. A betrayer of humanity, he hurt many people.

Saul might be described as a religious man without much of a soul. In a subsequent chapter, we will explore more fully what the soul is. For now, let's use this definition: Our soul is the place of deepest awareness where we are in touch with both the physical and spiritual worlds.

A master of form, Saul was out of touch with content. He wore his convictions like others put on clothing in the morning. Dressed well, his soul went naked. Saul's vengeful, violent actions were completely contrary to what any good Jew knew was clearly in the Torah. He was a whirling dervish—out of touch with his center.

But while Saul was off on one of his vendettas of self-righteousness, his eyes were truly opened when he was confronted by a brilliant light that left him physically blind. Those around him weren't really sure what had occurred, but Saul realized he had been at war with God. When he marvelously recovered his ability to see, he knew that he had found the Messiah. The effect was so profound that he had to change his name to Paul in order to convey his new identity. He became totally convinced that God, rather than Saul, was truly running the world. The Holy One could be trusted, and He would use the tragic situations of life for new purposes. All of this became clear to Paul as he recognized that God had revealed Himself and His purposes in the life, death, and resurrection of Jesus of Nazareth. Because of this revelation, Paul found a new basis for facing tragedy and making sense out of unmerited suffering.

When Saul was blinded on the Damascus road, he recovered his inner sight. Recognizing Jesus of Nazareth for who He truly was, Saul also discovered his own identity on the most fundamental level. Saul became Paul because his true personhood was released in his soul. From that point on, he could not only face suffering, but give it a constructive place in his life.

During a particularly difficult period he wrote this advice to his friends in Rome that we must explore: "We know that in everything God works for good with those who love Him, who are called according to His purpose."[1]

Significantly, he and the people to whom he was writing were living through a time of great injustice and political tyranny. Many died as innocent victims. Far from clear that they would be winners when history tabulated the results, it seemed Christ's followers were actually victims being crushed by forces of imperial power, social intolerance, and indiscriminate evil. Moreover, they lived in a time of ravaging illness without anesthetics or antiseptics. His text within this context is either pretext or a pledge of a wonderful source of consolation.

Under similar circumstances, most of us are far more apt to wonder if God works in anything for any purpose. Hard times often make us feel that God has deserted us. This sense of abandonment is an almost insurmountable experience for a child, and adults don't fare any better when they feel forsaken by God. Seemingly worse than death, the sensation leaves us stranded and adrift in the face of a descending tidal wave of despair. Everything in us hopes we are wrong and the apostle is right.

Was he?

IS ANYBODY THERE?

The answer to the question "Is anybody there?" makes a world of difference. Our task is not only to find the truth but grasp its application.

Surely great honesty and tenacity will be required, but the possibilities are worth the effort. We must find out whether the night is empty—or whether darkness only obscures what is quietly there.

Shortly before he killed himself, Ernest Hemingway gave us his final opinion. He wrote, "I live in a vacuum that is as lonely as a radio tube when the batteries are dead and there is no current to plug into." Earlier he had written a short story expressing his nihilistic view of life entitled, "A Clean, Well Lighted Place." Running through the story is the phrase, "Our Nada En Nada." Playing on words in the Lord's Prayer, the translation from Spanish means "Our Nothing who art in nothing." Hemingway had rejected any possibility of God being there. I respect the pain and despair that his final statements reflect. Abandonment has awesome power to destroy the human spirit. But while Hemingway struggled with manic-depression, his faithless life was a dead end path.[2]

I always admired this great writer's gusto and bravado. And yet as I look at pictures of him kneeling beside fierce animals he hunted just to kill, I wonder if he was not trying to control staggering fears that had taken up residence in his soul when he lost his capacity to believe.

Many people would be surprised to know that Hemingway's father was a close personal friend of the great evangelist, Dwight L. Moody. In fact, Hemingway had once been deeply concerned about his relationship with God. As a young journalist on the *Kansas City Star*, he wrote to his mother, "Don't worry or cry or fret about me being a good Christian. I am just as much as ever, and I pray every night and believe just as hard. . . . I believe in God and Jesus Christ, have hopes for a hereafter. . . ."

Yet, as he struggled with the cruelty and suffering caused by war, his stories began to reflect a bitter disillusionment. In *The Sun Also Rises*, he included an epigraph from Gertrude Stein, "You are all a lost generation." As he aged, Hemingway became increasingly distant from his friends and almost stopped communicating at all. He was described as having come to live inside a bad dream. Finally Hemingway turned into the embodiment of F. Scott Fitzgerald's description of life: "We beat on, boats against the current, borne back ceaselessly into the past."[3]

These are the words of brilliant minds who lost their souls. They are the conclusions of people who no longer believed Anyone was there. Having gained fame, wealth, and affluence, their lives ended as emotional scrap iron.

Should suffering similarly strip us of faith and obliterate the path to the soul, we face an identical frightening road. No, we must not let despair overtake us when night falls.

Therefore, our journey together starts with the hardest issue and the most devastating feeling that suffering imparts. Many times I have stood in a hospital corridor or the visitation room of a mortuary as people cried out, "Where is God?" Sometimes I have wanted to run as they sob despairingly, "Doesn't he care about what's happened to us?" But we must begin with such feelings, or we can't believe that anything can be worked out in our worst situations.

So how does "Saul-turned-Paul" know? Why is he so sure that we aren't abandoned?

THE LOUDEST EXPLOSIONS COME IN THE QUIETEST TIMES

This book is for those middle of the night experiences which can come in the midst of the day. Sooner or later everyone has such moments. For some it is a matter of a few days or nights, while for others, the twilight will last a lifetime—or so it will seem. During these times we desperately reach out, trying to find something solid to which to cling.

I invite you to join me on a journey through night toward a distant horizon where light always beckons. I offer you the stuff of my own personal discoveries as well as what others have found. During the period that I was making many of these discoveries, I found myself being awakened night after night at two or three o'clock. There were days I felt that lack of sleep would be my demise.

When volcanic eruptions in the soul are breaking forth, they seem to wait for the darkest times of night. In times of catastrophic change, we often don't get the full backwash until we close our eyes.

Whether the problem is death, divorce, devastation, personal failure, or the result of being in therapy, we can't solve our problems simply by picking up new rational explanations for them. We have to live through the emotional consequences. That's the hardest part. Generally other people not only don't understand, frequently they misunderstand and misinterpret. So we may feel paranoid and alienated. I found this isolation made it even harder to face the loneliest hours.

During one of those nights, I got up and started reading the Bible. Picking up a pencil, I began translating Psalm 56 into personal terms. My personal paraphrase helped me so I kept my scribblings in my Bible for a long time. When I began writing these pages, I found those lines helped me recall many discoveries that I had made in the dark. In subsequent chapters, this text is going to help guide us. Here's my personalized version:

O Lord, don't abandon me.
For heaven's sake, don't do what "they" have done to me!

I have been stepped on, oppressed, and arrogantly attacked. I even have former friends who now only wait to hurt me.

No matter where I turn, they are watching to see how they can damage my reputation. These enemies of my soul are always distorting my best intentions.

I don't want to be paranoid, but if I were unable to trust in you and your Word, I would be without hope!

Nevertheless, in my darkest nights, I am comforted because I know that you are keeping count of every time I turn in my sleep. Not even a single tear has been in vain, but you are keeping them all stored in your bottle.

I am so thankful that your bookkeeping includes a record of my pain.

Since I can trust you so completely, I remind myself that I can quit worrying about my detractors. If I will discipline my mind, I won't even have to think about all of the confusion around me and the uncertainty within.

Rather, I want to concentrate on thanking you for this time in my life.

Because you have already delivered me from the finality of the effects of death (which is the worst that could happen), everything else can be handled.

So, I know that you won't let me make a fool of myself.

Even when I don't see it, your light is certainly always there!

So be it!

I think this psalm can help give us stability and nourish our souls as we travel together.

27

So in this book I have gathered up the shavings and scraps that have fallen under the workbench as I and others have toiled to reconstruct the broken pieces of life. Together we will strive to understand our souls and why they are so necessary to us. We will also explore the strange, amazing Bible promises which pledge that God will work good for those who love Him.

Rather than trying to make a logical assault on the haunting questions that invade our minds during bad times, I hope to carve out a few handholds in the side of the pit that seems to swallow people. Often finding one's way out is just a matter of being able to find the next place to stand when there is no light. Stepping stones are generally more helpful than answer sheets when life's lamps have been extinguished.

FINDING THE PATH

We began with the story of June and Heather. Those eight days in which June lost her husband and her child were an embodiment of all of the tragic contradictions that invade human experience. Six years after the fatal afternoon when Heather died, June shared her difficult journey with me.

Any misgiving that there might not be a God working behind the visible scenes of the universe had not occurred to her. June had not struggled with a fear of abandonment in an empty world. Her questions were much more frightening. Was it possible that the world was in the hands of a cruel, capricious tyrant? What kind of God tells you one day that He loves you and then on the next takes your child?

In the first stage of her pilgrimage were nights spent screaming at God, venting the fury of her anger, "Who are you? Why did you kill my baby?" Again and again, overwhelming waves of bitterness spilled out as June accused God of leaving her at the moment she needed Him most. Anger, pain, and fear covered June's soul like a plastic bag over a child's face.

And yet. Yet—all of her assaults bumped up against

that other memory of a Wednesday morning filled with divine Love. She could not deny the incredible effect that encounter had had on her life. In one tear-flooded moment in June's car she had known the inner assurance of the love of God. Life-giving atmosphere was given to her. Far more than personal affirmation or even assurance of the reality of a Divinity, a new identity had been imparted, giving June self-worth that she had never known was possible. Even in the midst of rejection by her husband, June knew that she had personal value of incalculable worth. Instantly, she had realized her mistakes could not then nor in the future diminish her self-esteem and eternal value. With the passing of the months, insight began to take shape. June felt that she could not worship a God who wasn't truly in control of His creation. So if He were the Master of all destiny, why was the world filled with tragedies? June came to see that she had to come to grips with the idea that God might allow hurtful situations that He did not necessarily want or cause. But why would He let what was not intended happen? Her question had no answer.

Nevertheless, June's memories of love began to open a new pathway through her thinking. Love, not indifference, was the attribute of God that she realized made the most sense to explore. Through discussions, praying, and flashes of insight, a startling conclusion began to evolve. Could it be that because of and not in spite of her daughter's death, she was discovering how constant the love of God had always been?

Her mind went back and forth between the manger in the Nativity and the Cross on Good Friday. June began to think of the Crucified One as God's baby boy. Heather had died during a controlled coma that kept her from the pain and ravages of a nightmare death. In contrast, God the Father had watched His Son beaten, stripped, and humiliated. Then His life had agonizingly drained away through the most painful of deaths—completely for others.

"One evening," June told me quietly, "I realized that as much as I loved my child, I would never have let her die, and certainly I wouldn't let her die for anybody else. Yet the Christian message is that God the Father has such inconceivable love that He allowed His Son to go through hell for me. He remained silent as the One who was dearest to His heart was offered up for us. I don't understand all the theology, but an amazing idea became clear to me. The Creator of the universe was using my love for my daughter to teach me about the loving relationship He wanted to have with me."

"Can you understand why Heather died?" I asked.

"No," her eyes immediately became misty. "I still cannot understand why my child died. But," June continued with more resolve, "I do know that my discovery of God's love on that Wednesday morning was not to mock or confuse me. If I had not had that experience, I would have killed myself Friday night. Even though much of the time I wasn't in touch with His constant care, I now know that only His grace carried me through the funeral and on to the life I now have."

June's life is extremely productive today. Finishing her master's degree in counseling, she has developed an extraordinary ability to help others who struggle with tragedy. Her tears have been kept in His bottle.

"When you look back over those long hard years filled with feelings of isolation, do you think that you were ever abandoned by God?" I asked. Her reply was quiet but certain.

"No."

SOME STARTLING CONCLUSIONS

Suffering is generally the result of at least four possibilities: God, evil, ourselves, or a world that is imperfect and incomplete. It is seldom clear from whence came the wind that blew our house down. Regardless of where we place the blame or give the credit, the real issue is how we will use what has happened to us. When we decide that we will be transformed even if circumstances can't be changed, we have started to find our way out of the dimness.

Sometimes our problem is the result of a combination of all four influences. Rather than getting lost in what we may never sort out, I've found that if I look for a pattern working toward good within me, it is there. Like the underside of a beautiful needlepoint, I may see only knotted threads and random confusing shapes. Yet from above, from the divine perspective, God is creating in and through my life a work of art. His creation is called my soul.

There is hope during times of confusion and bewilderment that I can carry on even if the situation seems torturous. From the shores of Galilee, Jesus taught us to pray, "Our Father who art in heaven." I am assured that He is watching while I am waiting.

From the Cross of Calvary, Jesus also showed us that we can pray, "Our Father who art with us in our suffering." I can believe He is with me while I struggle. Nothing can separate us from Him.

DO
WE KNOW
THAT IN
EVERYTHING
GOD
WORKS
FOR
GOOD?

2

WHAT ARE THE ENEMIES OF MY SOUL?

O Lord, don't abandon me.

For heaven's sake, don't do what "they" have done to me!

I have been stepped on, oppressed, and arrogantly attacked. I even have former friends who now only wait to hurt me. No matter where I turn, they are watching to see how they can damage my reputation. These enemies of my soul are always distorting my best intentions (Ps. 56).

The enemies of my soul are the most deadly of all.

Regardless of the calamity that befalls us, ultimately the meaning of what has happened is a far greater problem than the experience itself. From deep within the recesses of our minds arise quandaries that can kill our spirits. Enemies like confusion, despair, and bitterness spring into life. Before we go further, we must identify the destroyers that lurk along the path and wait to push their way into our lives. We may be tempted to believe people are our problem. Actually, we tend to see in our persecutors what is gnawing on our own souls.

These devourers of the human spirit are difficult to handle because their logic is so natural and reasonable. Generally they emerge as inner aids, offering protection against further emotional assault. Their answers seem justifiable and valid. At first they offer us comfort with simple, shallow clichés. Then they remind us that unless we take care of ourselves, no one else will. Finally, they unpack their luggage filled with malignancy and melancholy. In the end they allow no room in our mental houses for any others but themselves. Because these

WHEN THE NIGHT IS TOO LONG

nemeses are creatures of darkness, they finally draw the shades and shut out all other light. Yes, they make the night both darker and longer.

We must make sure that entrance is denied to these unseen opponents that want to live within our souls. Unless we win that battle, all else is lost. We must identify our adversaries and hold the door shut while we keep the candles of hope lit. I want to introduce you to three of the most destructive of these forces and the questions that will predictably invite their entry.

I am going to suggest that we initially tend to ask the wrong questions during times of suffering. I am going to show you how we can change the destructive questions into constructive ones.

Let's begin by examining one of the most subtle of these spiritual enemies. Learn to recognize the inimical invader named Confusion.

CONFUSION

"Why Has This Happened to Me?"

I warn you that Confusion first appears in a most deceptive form. Seemingly disheveled and in total disarray, his disconnected demeanor is a complete facade. As a matter of fact, Confusion is an efficiency expert. He knows how to gather up all of our accumulated knowledge and experiences and in the shortest amount of time reduce their collective meaning to nonsense. While he appears to move aimlessly, actually he is carefully scrambling all of the data we carry in our heads until what we know becomes quite useless. Nourished by gossip and rumor, he uses suspicion as a primary tool in causing distortion. Once he has created paranoia, our soul is in deep trouble.

Confusion first appears when we cannot make sense out of what has befallen us. He poses one particularly difficult question. "Why has this happened to me?" When we cannot find an adequate or satisfactory answer, the work of Confusion begins. Therefore, it is of critical importance that we face this question with confidence.

"Why me? Why us?" a young mother asked sadly. "All we ever wanted was a child that we could love and cherish. And now look at what we have." Maggie and I bent over to peer into the windows of the incubator, squinting to see the tiny baby with tubes running in every direction, who was slowly turning purple even as we talked. "We tried so hard for so long to have a baby." Her tone of voice revealed the desperation of many years of frustration. "We truly believed the hand of God brought this pregnancy to pass. So why is it now ending because of carelessness?"

While running an amniocentesis test, the doctor had punctured the placenta and caused a hemorrhage. Although the hospital had reacted immediately, the damage was irreversible. We both knew that within a few hours, this premature infant would be gone.

With confusion in her eyes Maggie asked again, "Why me?" Obviously she felt deeply and profoundly betrayed.

I must tell you in all candor—there is no complete answer to her question. The best we have is the tabulation of the results of cause and effect that chemistry, physics, and psychology offer. However, our hearts want a response that is satisfying.

Why did it happen? On one level the answer is obvious. A needle was stronger than tissue and when the membrane broke, blood pressure created a hemorrhage. The doctor made a mistake.

Why the car wreck? Well, when tons of metal fly out of control toward a metal post, the speed creates a deadly impact. The road was slick.

Why the stroke at age forty? Aneurysms can only last so long and then the elasticity of the blood vessel snaps when the blood pressure is too great. The body proved fragile.

Will any of those answers speak to the nagging fears of the heart and satisfy the deepest levels of the soul?

Not a hair!

"Why?" can often be answered with biological facts, formulas, equations from physics, or psychological studies about why people do crazy things. But very seldom can "why?" be answered so completely that the heart is relieved and the soul consoled. No, our query is wrong.

We must change the question. Paul actually turned *why* into a *what*. He implied that the better inquiry is, "What can happen if I turn the whole matter over for God to use?" Once people begin to look for some positive use for their devastation, Confusion can be converted into creativity.

In turning away from the whys, well over half of the battle against Confusion is won. The first step is to begin seeking an avenue of expression that will allow what has happened to be used for a constructive purpose. At this moment that idea may seem totally impossible, emotionally inappropriate, and physically inconceivable, but I assure you it is not.

In fact, I want to introduce you to friends who are living examples of turning tragedy into triumph. George and Carol Faulk illustrate what I am describing.

Their son, John, and Tate, our youngest son, were the same age and were best friends. The boys' temperaments were well suited to make them real buddies. Before Tate left for summer camp, he and John had planned a special outing. Their plans were to remain forever unfulfilled. Late in the afternoon before Tate's return, John had a heart seizure and died in the swimming pool.

When Tate's bus pulled in, we had to greet him with the terrible news. Brokenhearted and overwhelmed with grief, we left the parking lot immediately to try to bring comfort to our friends. In complete shock, Tate sat in the front seat mumbling, "Why? Why? Why?"

But the next chapter in the story is even more painful. One year later John's younger brother, Colby, was climbing a rope in the physical education class at school. Suddenly he slumped forward and crumpled to the floor. Even before the ambulance arrived, the teachers knew Colby was gone. Once more our neighborhood, stunned into absolute silence, gathered around a grave. Some speculated that the whole of the universe had betrayed this family.

During the years that followed, I watched George and Carol climb out of the ashes. Whether they were aware of it or not, they began to build a living monument to their children by pouring their love and concern into people who were smitten by tragedy. Refusing any form of self-pity, they looked continually to the needs of others. Through their efforts, a new group began to emerge in our community: Compassionate Friends, composed of bereaved parents who offer consolation and friendship to other grieving couples. In the ensuing years hundreds of broken parents have found help because George and Carol looked for a way to use their pain. What might have been bitter confusion has been used to bring clarity to others who were devastated. The inner enemy was thwarted.

Why must be turned into *what*.

The first question to ask in times of suffering is: What can happen if I turn the whole matter over to God to use? Now let's turn to the next question that must be faced and confront another enemy of our soul.

DESPAIR

"Where Is God When Disaster Strikes?"

The question invites another enemy that lurks in the shadows waiting to attack: Despair. This antagonist is a reprehensible maggot who lives by devouring hope. A worm-like creature, he begins to bore into our hearts when we are feeling hopeless and dejected. At first he lies dormant while we explore various alternatives to our difficult situation. However, as easy answers and trite clichés fail, Despair emerges from the larva stage and prepares to crawl into our dreams and confidence. Quickly he chews away the props and aids which have sustained us in other difficult days. Before we are aware, he has undercut the support system that gives us strength. As inevitable discouragements mount, Despair remains hidden, feeding his ravishing appetite.

However, he is growing within like a rampaging cancer, boring his way from the heart to the mind. The parasite's ultimate destination is the nerve center of our faith. Once he cuts through and devours the presuppositions by which we have lived, he has gained complete control over our perspective. At that point we will truly believe that we have been abandoned by God. The universe becomes a vacuum.

Despair has eaten enormous holes in the pages of the history of the twentieth century. He has consumed the prevailing optimism that characterized the plans and dreams of politicians and philosophers in the early decades.

Believing World War I would end all wars, by 1950 their grand designs had turned sour. The barbarism of World War II produced pessimism which settled into the soul of a majority of the academic and intellectual community. The specter of Facism, Nazism, Communism, the Holocaust, the potential of nuclear termination of all life, a deadly narrow rationalism, and a loss of confidence in the moral character of world leaders culminated in a crisis of faith in the Western world. Vietnam and the fall of Nixon signaled the death of political innocence for America. The low came in the late sixties with the emergence of the "God is Dead" theology, proclaiming a total loss of any sense of divine presence in this world. The so-called "moral revolution" that followed only demonstrated how people can become irresponsible when they no longer recognize any absolutes guiding their behavior. Despair had succeeded. The whirlwind of change had invited an all-consuming disillusionment about the future. Where was God? Seemingly none could answer. The lack of an explanation was disastrous for multitudes of people who felt betrayed by life.

As mushrooms grow best in manure and darkness, so Despair flourishes in the absence of light and insight. Such a social backdrop of hopelessness has made personal disasters all the more treacherous. If God is gone, then consolation vanishes.

So the issue is not "where," but *can I recognize how*

He is present to me right now? We must develop an inner perception that recognizes what our sensory system cannot record.

Despair must be exorcised. This vicious enemy of our soul must be dispelled so that warmth can replace the chill that grips the soul. How can this be done?

Again, Paul implies that we are asking the wrong question. "Where" isn't the right query. The quest for locating God keeps us from recognizing the solution that is already at hand. During a debate with the best philosophers of Athens, Paul found they were pessimistic about the possibility of finding God. He astonished these intellectuals of his time by telling them the one true God was never far from any of us.

Today the Apostle might have decided to hold his debate at a very different place. Perhaps he would have gone to Oxford, Harvard, or Berkeley to argue with those who have decided there is no potential for God existing in this universe. Possibly he might have traveled to Hollywood to talk with screenplay writers who describe a world without purpose, depicting only empty relationships and betrayed trust. It is conceivable that he might have chosen to stand on a corner of New York City's Times Square to assault the world of sleaze and pornography. There he would stand toe-to-toe with vendors of smut who have sold their souls to the god of sensuality. His message would be the same in each instance. Having eyes, they no longer see. The condition is not one of the optic nerve, but a disease of the soul.

Paul's words are still our answer: "In Him we live and move and have our being." Like the atmosphere that surrounds us, the very air we breathe, and the thoughts that appear in our minds, He is always in our midst. Or more pointedly, we are always in *His* midst.

So the issue is not "where," but "How can I recognize He is present to me right now?" We must learn to develop an inner perception that recognizes what our sensory system cannot record. Eyes, ears, and touch receive only partial readings of reality. However, we can develop an inner knowing that is able to reach the larger realities that are spiritual. Although lost by many people in the twentieth century, our soul is that part of us that can see the unseen. Once it is recovered, we have a way to fight Despair.

The soul is the center of perceptiveness for the Divine. An area of extraordinary sensitivity, the soul can be so ignored, brutalized, or depleted that it no longer seems to function. Fear, doubt, abandonment, pain, anxiety, and failure can slowly but surely shut us down until there is only hollowness at the center. Our loss of the sense of the presence of God will be in proportion to the degree to which our soul has become stunted and shriveled.

Often we have to begin at some very human places in order to quicken our spiritual awareness and start the soul fully functioning again. Perhaps it will surprise you to read that often I and others have begun this work by looking in seemingly very nonreligious places. Through the years one of the most significant touchstones for me has been the arts. Great music, painting, sculpture, and architecture remind me that there is beauty in this world that no amount of ugliness can obscure. The greatest of human creations all point beyond themselves to a Creator who has not stopped working.

When I hear great compositions like Handel's "Hallelujah Chorus," I am profoundly reminded that a celebration of God continues at the center of all reality.

When I look at the paintings of some of my favorite artists like Rico LaBrun, Andrew Wyeth, or John Pike, I realize that even the most common settings are endowed with profound beauty.

When I read books by writers like Boris Pasternak, Fedor Dostoevsky, Shalom Alecheim, and Harper Lee, I am compelled to remember that behind all the complexities of human existence, there is still a Divine design at work. Wonderful artistic creations all demand that I look again, trying to see with the inner eye. They restore my soul.

The Bible often uses streams, rivers, and oceans as a

metaphor to describe the work of God. Why? Because the vastness and hiddenness of the sea remind us that God is often silently but securely there in the deepest places of human experience.

When I lived in California, a stroll along the beaches always heightened my sense of God's presence. The waves rolling up from the deep resonated with my own inner depths. Across the road from my present office is a large lake that contains the same secrets for restoring calm. As the psalmist once wrote, "Out of the depths have I cried to thee."

I must also confess that in the innocence, the beauty, and the warmth of babies and children I always find promise that a wondrous goodness is still here. The eyes of little children convey an assurance that everything in creation really did begin with inherent virtue. The wonder of the child is a constant reminder to me of the heavenly Father's presence.

When I become disillusioned with adults, I have a conversation with my four-year-old granddaughter who calls me Abba. I'll call California and say, "Guess who?"

"I know it's you, Abba," she will giggle.

"No, no," I will protest. "I am Santa Claus calling to check on whether Rachael Wise is being a good girl."

"I know it's you, Abba," she insists.

"Well," I try to imitate a rotund deep voice. "Wouldn't you rather talk to Santa Claus than Abba?"

"Oh, no," her little voice says brightly, "because I like my Abba better than Santa Claus."

At which time I say, "Child, your education is assured" (though she has no idea what I'm talking about!).

After spending some time talking with Rachael, I find it much easier to believe in goodness again. The cynicism and bleakness of daily life seem to slip away as we discuss important matters like Jemima Puddle-Duck and Br'er Rabbit. She helps me look again for how God is at work.

There's another place where soul can be recovered. When suffering and goodness meet, we are often surprised by how much of the presence of God arises out of the mix. Caring people can turn emptiness into fullness. Let me share how I saw this happen.

In my book, *When There Is No Miracle*, I related a personal experience that I want to fully explain. Extremely serious kidney surgery was required for our six-year-old son, Todd. As he came out from under the anesthesia, the pain was enormous. Trying to help him, we were constantly distracted by the crying of a child down the hall. I rang for a nurse and complained that our child's problems were being increased because someone was not attending whomever was two doors down.

The nurse apologetically explained that a child named Richard was suffering from third degree burns from his neck down to his heels. His father's car had struck a gasoline truck. The father burned to death in the explosion while the child barely escaped with his life. His mother was unable to help because she was immobilized in shock. Because the family did not have funds for a private nurse and the hospital was understaffed, Richard was often left unattended.

"I'm very sorry," the nurse said with genuine concern. "Really it would not take a great deal to stop his crying. The burns have been impregnated with gauze and as they heal, they are drawing up. Richard is crying because the itching is intense. If someone were available to just touch his wounds, he would be able to go to sleep immediately."

I was shocked as I thought of the implications. "Would you allow anyone to help?" I asked.

"Sure," she replied. "We're just as troubled by the child's crying as you are."

Immediately the youth group at the church came to mind. I knew that most of these teenagers had experienced little contact with human suffering. This could be an opportunity for them to help the little boy and at the same time become sensitized to human need. Calls were made and quickly round-the-clock teenage teams were formed to stay in Richard's room to relieve his pain. When the itching began, they would gently touch his back until he could fall asleep. Within a few days the critical period passed, and Richard was on his way to full recovery. Of course, my own son was doing much better, and the teenagers had been part of an experience that would probably always remind them of their potential to help suffering people. The matter seemed settled. Then Richard's mother came to the hospital.

Slowly the grief had worn away enough that she was able to face reality. With her world completely cratered, she was still struggling. The nurse had sent her to our room when she inquired about who had taken care of her child. Apparently the boy had talked enthusiastically about his new friends. By the time she knocked on our door, she had pieced the story together.

"Thank you," she said with tears in her eyes. "I cannot tell you what this kindness has meant to us. My son is so much better. . . ." There was a long pause. Then she added, "*I* have been helped. During these past days I thought God had forsaken us. But now I know that He will truly help us when we cannot help ourselves."

In the midst of her tragedy, she had begun to believe that God was still working with her family. I find that remembering how many, many people are constant sources of goodness, mercy, and kindness changes my perception of being deserted. Pain actually becomes the opportunity to recognize how God is working. Despair is repelled and hope returns. A little time spent with one of these earthly angels has often helped me get back in touch with the heavenly Father.

Where must be turned into *how*.

I've found that the second question I must ask in times of suffering is: Can I recognize how God is present to me right now? Let's look at another question that often haunts us and expose the next villain.

BITTERNESS

"When Will I Be Vindicated?"

Bitterness grows and reproduces best in the brackish backwaters of memories filled with the residue of injustice and betrayal. Hurt feelings, unresolved slights, and wounds that have never healed, fester and ferment in a swamp of acrimony. Like rancid, cold dishwater saturated with the grease and garbage of yesterday's dirty dishes, Bitterness stains and soils everything that once was fresh and clean. It leaves a greasy coating that contaminates every thought and emotion.

Our best intentions are left smudged and ruined. The taste of Bitterness lingers in the mouth, ruining the savor of the sweet things of life. When we feel that we have been stepped on, oppressed, or arrogantly attacked, we become prime targets for Bitterness. As a swamp generates malaria, betrayal breeds Bitterness.

So much tragedy has nothing whatever to do with God. People are the problem. Recently I ran into an old college classmate who was surprised to learn that I had gone into the ministry. He remarked, "It must be really difficult to serve God!" Reflecting for a moment, I was surprised to hear my own answer, "No, serving God isn't so hard; it's serving people that can get painful."

Sartre's cynical play, *No Exit*, depicted how a relationship can be a place of torment. Apparently Sartre's own boat got stuck in the sludge. He is right that former friends can create bitterness as can no other source.

But what if we have been genuinely betrayed? What if, in the maze of confusion, one conclusion is certain: We were truly sold out. The burden is infinitely increased. There is no pain comparable to that which comes from a destroyed relationship. When business partners deal treacherously, spouses fail, children utterly disappoint, and friends become disloyal, we are truly set adrift in a world that is empty and hostile. Only those who have faced such moments of isolation can fully appreciate the vacuum that lost trust creates. In that void Bitterness marches unobstructed.

I had assumed an eternal friendship with a person that I had known for most of my ministry. Having worked through most of the crises of this person's adult life, I knew that in a moment of desperate need, I could ask for help and counsel. Caught in a serious dilemma, I poured out very private and confidential information, knowing that of all people, I could count on the loyalty and support of my friend. In the ensuing months, I was to discover that what I had related in pain and secret was being repeated to others. As the facts slowly surfaced, I realized that the problem I faced was now compounded by the gossip that my "friend" had "confidentially" shared with others. The words of the psalmist began to take flesh: "They are watching to see how they can damage my reputation. These enemies of my soul are always distorting my best intentions." How does one ever fully recover from such discoveries? It's not easy, but that is exactly our task.

In our minds there seem to be ledgers that will not be satisfied until all the debts of injustice have been appeased. We hunger to know that when the bottom line is drawn, we will have received full credit for our pain. The need for exoneration causes "When?" to leap up out of our souls. If there is no answer, our question settles back into dismal waters to soak in more bitterness. Incalculable masses of people have prayed again and again, "How long, O Lord? When will we be vindicated?"

Interestingly enough, Paul did not struggle with this question. Rather than worrying about the possibility of exoneration, he proclaimed that God is at work establishing His purposes. To avoid bitterness, the Apostle seems to have believed that we must get beyond our personal preoccupations and become centered in the will of God. Rather than seeking exoneration, our hope must be placed in the Person of the heavenly Father Himself. Only in Him can satisfaction be found.

The Apostle's faith was grounded in conviction about the sovereignty of God. Abandoning the quest for absolution, he placed his confidence in the belief that the divine process would itself be the source of consolation. Rather than looking inward or outward, he looked upward.

Paul turned the "when" into "Who." *"Who is God?"*

45

was his question. He avoided Bitterness because he could answer the "who" question by remembering at least three characteristics of the personality of God.

1. Paul had no doubt that the heavenly Father knows what is happening. He believed that God troubled Himself with the most common and banal of human affairs.

2. The apostle had no doubt that God has the power to change things. He knew that God was able.

3. Paul had no question that God loves us. The trouble-filled environment called life is still permeated by His love.

Paul believed that we can count on these facts to always be true. Our hope and help lies in who God is.

While it may be difficult, Paul tells me that I can dare to forget about my vindication. If I give up the demand for a time and place for balance to be achieved, I will discover that God's ultimate purposes are all encompassing and satisfying. The issues of personal acquittal must be left in His hands. He is able to do more than I could ever guess.

The final question to ask in times of injustice and inequity is: Who is God?

CONCLUSIONS

When our best intentions have been distorted and we are being arrogantly attacked, we must remember that our only real danger comes from unseen enemies that lie in wait to attack our souls. Regardless of the tragedy, we have to recall that what has happened is never as significant as how we receive its effect. We stand or fall on the basis of how the internal warfare is waged.

The issue that churns within the soul is the quest for meaning. The answers that arise out of Scripture suggest purpose. Finding and recovering the purposes of God is the source of all hope. Asking *why*, *where*, and *when* only leads us down dead-end paths. Changing the questions to *what*, *how*, and *who* will bring us resolution and direction. Here's a new set of questions for you to

WHAT ARE THE ENEMIES OF MY SOUL?

use in your battle against Confusion, Despair, and Bitterness.

- WHAT can happen if I turn the whole matter over to God for His use?
- HOW can I recognize God's presence right now?
- WHO is true God and what is His nature really like?

Recently a dear friend, Jan Wolfard, died at the age of thirty-eight. Jan had done a great deal of typing for me over the years, and I had helped her with a serious mental illness, triggered by the failure of her marriage. Her steep climb back to stability had been long, hard, and very courageous. Few people with the severity of her illness ever come so far. Jan's conviction about the presence of God in her life was the source of encouragement that kept her from capitulating to despair. A poem found in her belongings conveyed her answer.

> Lord,
> May I settle it once and for all
> that I am dealing directly with you.
> You need never apologize
> for any plan you ordain for me
> since nothing but good
> can come from your hand.
> You are sufficient
> for every changing circumstance
> in my God-planned life—
> for every unchanging circumstance
> as well.[1]

We can pray this prayer with confidence. He does work in everything.

GOING IN TO COME OUT

Everyone needs a sense of how the image of God is imprinted on their life. If we can discover our uniqueness, we will begin to deal with pain as Jesus Christ did. Here's the opportunity.

Have you ever considered keeping a journal? One's most intimate thoughts and reflections are recorded in these secret books. Often just trying to record what we can't fully understand brings new clarity and insight. Going back and reading what we wrote has an amazing way of bringing additional understanding. During the next several weeks, I want you to use the problems in your life as the basis on which you write about how the nature of God has been a part of who you are. We will attempt to discover how problems can perfect us and bring us to completion.

Parenthetically, I suggest that you decide right now where you will hide your journal. I keep mine in a vault under a water bed, which is guarded by ten alligators who spit radioactive bullets at anyone who gets within twenty feet. You need to know that this book is secure so you can be completely honest in what you write. If you leave it around, you can bet someone will happen on to it—and journals do make extraordinarily interesting reading.

On the first page put the heading, "Regressing." Your first assignment is to go backward and look at how you have developed to this point. You can get lost in such a search so for the moment confine your probing to two key issues. First, what is genuine in me? When I look back over the years, what do I see that is good, true, honest, authentic, and abiding? What can I find which might have the touch of God upon it? Far from arrogance, we all need to be aware of what is right within us. Many times in your life you have reflected the image of God without even knowing it. Bring those times into your awareness. Perhaps you will discover ways in which God has been with you that you have missed recognizing.

Next, explore the question, what is false in me? As I discovered the good, where did I also find the bad? Where has my behavior been phony, deceptive, hollow, unproductive, destructive, or defeating? What is there in me that really does need changing? Would I dare to ask God to rid me of these limitations? Could I begin to see how my present problems might be an opportunity for the rectification of these deficiencies? Your assignment is to write about these matters until you have a clear picture of your need.

After you have worked on these two areas for some time, try to condense your discoveries into two columns. Entitle the headings: The Image and The Distortion. Write one-word descriptions of your conclusions on the appropriate side. Don't do this quickly. Make sure each word is as accurate as possible.

DOES
GOD
KNOW
HOW HARD
AND
DARK
AND
DEEP
THE HURT
IS?

3

WHAT GOOD IS THERE IN SO MUCH BAD?

"I have been stepped on, oppressed, and arrogantly attacked" (Ps. 56).

Why does it hurt so much? Why do people suffer so often?

The answer lies in how we are made. There are components in the mind, body, and soul that make an encounter with pain inevitable. As the heart has a great faculty for feeling, so the soul or psyche has an insatiable desire for meaning. When these two sources of energy cross, the potential for profound joy or bottomless despair is created. Therein lies the dilemma with which everyone who is truly alive must contend. The price paid for the ability to experience elation is the potential to be devastated.

My dog doesn't have this problem. While she misses attention and surely gets upset if the dog bowl isn't filled regularly, there's no capacity for either profound bereavement or *joie de vivre*. When her puppies are given away, they're missed for a very short while, but if one is brought back a month or two later, there's no family reunion. In fact, the response is more likely to be hostility over the potential loss of territory. No, a dog is spared the pain of ever being betrayed and left at the altar. On the other hand, dogs have no sense of the meaning of their existence, either.

Why is this so? Why are we different? Because we are created in the image of God.

OUR CAPACITY TO CARE

The ultimate solution to the enigma surrounding pain is not in psychology or anthropology, but theology. We are like the caring God who created us. No one can avoid being affected by this divine-human paradox. The Bible begins with the affirmation that God created us like Himself. So, the answer to mysteries that often engulf us is not to be found in exploring our experience as much as it is in understanding God.

The problem is that the biblical viewpoint has gotten lost in the shuffle. History, philosophy, catastrophe, and general cultural confusion have ended in the malaise that we find in the Ernest Hemingways and F. Scott Fitzgeralds. Many still struggle to find their way between two points of view locked in confrontation.

Eternal Nothing

On one side are those who maintain that if there is a deity at all, He, She, or It is basically unknowable, impenetrable, uninvolved, and unconcerned. Comedian Woody Allen has put the issue to us satirically. In his film, *Stardust Memories*, Sandy Bates carries on an imaginary conversation with the Deity. Bates asks, "Why is there so much suffering?"

The Divinity responds, "This is unanswerable."

Trying again, Bates asks, "Is there a God?"

The voice says, "These are the wrong questions."

In Allen's version of *War and Peace* called *Love and Death*, he takes on the ultimate issue of tragedy. As Boris and a comrade walk over a battlefield strewn with bodies, the friend says, "God is testing us."

Boris replies, "If He is going to test us, why doesn't he give us a written exam?"

Allen's conclusion in his book, *My Philosophy, Getting Even*, is, "Eternal nothing is O.K. if you're dressed for it." So much for the possibility of getting in touch with God.

A Caring God

In contrast, Paul and his contemporaries proclaimed that God's nature is reflected in His involvement with the concerns and woes of both His creation and His created ones. Today multitudes believe that God is a personality who seeks relationships. The scandal of the biblical message is that we are fashioned by a God who has the capacity to hurt and to suffer. As surely as the potter puts his own creativity into the clay vessel, so the Creator has stamped His nature on us. Therefore, we cannot avoid the fact that we are made to feel deeply and to respond fully. Our humanness has built-in sensitivity as surely as we have eyes and ears. If this capacity to hurt, to feel, and to care should be lost, the very essence of our humanness also disappears. Those who have ceased to be able to hurt are either inhuman, mentally ill—or dead. Those who want to know why life can hurt so much must ponder the nature of the Creator and His creation because we are like our Father.

Paul came to understand how profoundly the nature of God and humanity are locked together. Moreover, he perceived that suffering always has the potential to release this divine dimension as nothing else can. Remember what he wrote? "We know that in everything God works for good with those who love Him, who are called according to His purpose."[1] This verse states his conviction that God is always working for good through our experiences. In the next sentence he says it is God's purpose to use all of our experiences to shape us to be like Him. Paul's conclusion was that we are ultimately "to be conformed to the image of Christ."

Rather than destroying us, the crucifying times actually can be the means by which our personalities are transformed into a true reflection of God's image. The suffering of Jesus Christ was the ultimate example of the capacity of God to use betrayal and brokenness as His opportunity for redemption and reconciliation. From the depths of pain can arise new life.

What is it to become fully human? Like a grinding stone polishing a diamond into brilliant luster, humanness is most completely expressed when abrasive, bruising blows of life result in a forgiving, gracious personality that is able to even love enemies.

Why do we hurt?

First, we are like God. We are creatures of great sensitivity.

Second, pain has the power to perfect us. We are made

to be vulnerable to its assault in order to become complete.

THE IMAGE EMERGES

Because the image of God tends to get hidden within the folds of human experience, we have to observe His love in others in order to see what it looks like. So I want to look at how our Godlikeness appears and expands in us. Let's ponder some practical expressions of how the *imago dei* emerges, emanates, and is expressed.

Let me tell you two stories about what it means to be a human being with the capacity to hurt. Both are remarkable examples of displaying the image of God.

Kitty Hart is an amazingly energetic woman with great drive. An X-ray technician, she has also raised two outstanding sons. Perhaps the most remarkable quality one discovers as Kitty talks is her energetic buoyancy and zest for living. Considering the extraordinary pain that has filled her life, her optimism is confounding. The fact that she is alive is itself something of a miracle.

As a teenage Jewish girl, Kitty and her family were torn apart by the Nazi assault that ripped her world to pieces. As her family struggled to survive annihilation, they were separated. She and her mother were shipped to Auschwitz Concentration Camp in Poland. Her father and brother disappeared.

Kitty discovered quickly that survival depended on doing daily jobs too nauseating to describe. Such tasks as carrying out buckets of human waste from latrines provided minimal shelter to keep winter ice storms from devouring her. Removing jewelry and other items from bodies being prepared for crematoriums gave her precious trinkets with which to bargain for bits of food. Being on a detail that spent the day throwing bodies onto wagons kept her out of the endless flow of human traffic toward the crematoriums. Kitty's adolescence was spent in pursuit of an existence that seems worse than death.

The horror of the murder of six million Jews is so overwhelming that statistics have persuaded many that people are essentially only animals. The Hitlers, Himmlers, Eichmanns, and Mengeles seem to prove the hypothesis that humanity is no more than the most cunning and dangerous of all species. The death camps suggest that survival of the fittest is a fact and the only measure of right in this universe. So the experience of Kitty Hart poses an unavoidable question for us. Can people really be a reflection of a God of love?

As the years dragged on, Kitty was subjected to horrors that only increased with time. During one period she worked in the infirmary. As the sick poured in, Kitty found old friends and relatives among the multitude. Reunions were a singular source of joy when she was able to smuggle in a crumb of bread or an article of clothing to help someone survive. On one of those bleak winter mornings, the commandant appeared, demanding that the entire infirmary be emptied into waiting trucks. Instantly everyone knew that meant death.

The influx of more and more Jews had produced an overload of sick people. The Nazi solution for the crowding was to exterminate the present population. Since none would survive anyway, recovering patients were only marking time until they disappeared. Kitty knew there was no alternative but to comply with the orders, which soldiers stood ready to enforce with club and bayonet. One by one she helped her friends out of the cold, shabby sick bay on their way to death. At such moments the terror and horror that mingled with overwhelming anger created a single desire. Should she survive, the day would come when she would avenge the butchery. Hate kept Kitty alive.

Even though the end of the war was at hand and the defeat of the Nazis had become imminent, Kitty and her mother were sent on a death march to another camp. All that kept her bleeding feet moving was the burning intention to get her hands on her German captors. Germans of any shape or size. Germans who would bleed and die as her people had. Germans who could be strangled.

On the final day of their imprisonment, Kitty and her

mother noticed that men in strange uniforms were walking outside the barbed wire. Then an S.S. guard appeared and announced surrender to the Allies. Immediately the prisoners turned on him, tearing his uniform from his body. As other inmates beat the man, Kitty saw his dagger fall to the ground. Instantly she grabbed the knife and ran for the gate out of the camp. Surging together, the prisoners rampaged into town seeking food. Kitty clutched at the dagger with one thought in mind. Somewhere she would find a German to try to even a score that could never be settled.

Breaking down the door to one of the village houses, they poured in seeking food. The house appeared empty until a prisoner noticed a door that went down to the basement. Quickly Kitty descended the stairs with the knife in the air, poised for attack. From out of the shadows the forms of people began to emerge. There they were. Germans who were trapped just as Kitty and her friends had been for all those years.

"Throw it!" someone yelled in her ear. "Stick them!"

As one man stepped from the group, Kitty drew her arm over her head ready to plunge the knife into his chest.

"Throw it!" the man behind her screamed.

With the blade overhead, a most contrary impulse surged up from her soul. An almost lost emotion touched her intention. Deep within the recesses of her mind, compassion arose. Unexpected goodness froze the knife in the air. Her obsession with revenge gave way to thoughts of forgiveness. To Kitty's amazement, her own hand turned, hurling the knife against a wall where it fell harmlessly to the floor.

"I realized that if I killed the man, the Nazis would have succeeded in making me like them," she now reflects.

By bearing humiliation and degradation with forgiveness, Kitty demonstrated that the inhumanity of the Nazis was only a momentary perversion of true humanness. Kitty is living proof that the image of God can be obscured, but not destroyed. The worst that life offers produced in her a transcendent quality of character.

Kitty found that she was changed by her decision. By exchanging benevolence for bestiality, she profited the most.

How can the effect of years filled with hate be reversed in a few moments of forgiveness? Nothing compares with the power of love. No cleansing agent, no scouring powder, no catharsis can accomplish what a few moments of absolution will do for the soul. The darkest depths of hate reveal most fully the highest possibilities of love. Human experience can hurt so much because our capacity for love is so great.

What do I learn from Kitty's example and situation? What happens to me is not as important as how I respond. Being created in the image of God, I always have the capacity to use the worst of experiences as the best opportunities for love. From hence the image emerges.

THE IMAGE EMANATES

Can we truly be a full expression of who God is? In fact, transformation follows when His image is flowing in and through us. We are changed; the people around us are changed. Often something in or about us must be cracked open for the inner reality to spring to life. Here's a story of a moment when a living portrait of God was painted in a family's living room.

Consider the experience of the Cardins. Having a great love for children, but unable to have their own, Paul and Barbara wanted to adopt. Fully aware of the complications, they elected to adopt older children who had been removed from their homes because of abuse. Attempting to communicate genuine love and unconditional acceptance to emotionally hurting children is, perhaps, the most demanding of all tasks.

On a Sunday in February, Paul and Barbara came to church thinking about how they were going to deal with a recurring disciplinary problem. They had decided to wait until after morning worship to tackle the emotionally explosive confrontation.

That morning I was speaking on unconditional love. Exploring how we could better recover the image of

God, I challenged each person to find a new and creative way to show unqualified affection. I ended by asking the congregation to pray for some new and innovative change in their capacity to care. Immediately after the prayer, an extraordinary idea occurred to Paul.

He began to ponder an aspect of the meaning of Christ's death on the cross that drastically changed what he had planned to do as punishment. The idea of Jesus taking our sin upon Himself became very personal and applicable. Earlier in the morning, he had concluded that the children needed to be spanked and isolated for a significant amount of time. Now Paul knew he must reverse his decision. He was to take the children's punishment for them. Paul would take the three licks and sit in the corner for two hours.

After the immediate inspiration of morning worship passed, Paul had second thoughts. After all, the Olympics were on television that afternoon, and maybe he could accomplish the same result by just commuting the punishment. Paul thought if he prayed, perhaps there would be some Divine indication that he could just forget the first idea. He prayed; nothing happened. With far less enthusiasm, he decided to follow his first sense of guidance.

After lunch he called a family conference. The infractions of the rules were fully discussed and the appropriate punishment announced. The children didn't protest their sentence as being unjust. Then Paul calmly announced that he would take the penalty upon himself. The children were dumbfounded and did not understand what he was saying. Calmly and with deepest sincerity, Paul explained he was only doing what Jesus had done by setting us free of the penalty of our sin and guilt. He told the children that while they probably did not understand fully what this action meant, he believed doing this would help because he loved them. The brother and sister could only stare.

While Paul could not see the children's faces as he struck himself with each lick, he could feel their astonishment. When he went to the corner, his daughter came over and hugged him. Then Paul began the long afternoon of staring at the wall and listening.

Immediately the children went to work. Realizing that Daddy was in the corner because they had been bad created instant motivation. In some way they wanted to make it up to him. They were slow and respectful when walking past him. While they were free to watch the Olympics, they seemed to feel that working was more appropriate. Paul found the harder the children worked, the more he wished they would simply rest and enjoy the afternoon. But he remained silent in the corner.

Eventually Paul became an embarrassment. Daddies aren't supposed to be punished. When the time was up, there were sincere thank yous and life went back to normal. But the children had seen and learned something that vastly exceeded anything they had ever experienced in their lives. More surprisingly, Paul found that something awesome had happened to him.

The experience of taking the punishment for the violation of his own rules had created and developed a new and profound awareness that Paul is still trying to understand. Previously he had experienced suffering with and because of his children. However, self-imposed suffering was a very different matter. He said to me, "Ironically, the punishment makes me love more deeply now."

As Paul talked about the meaning of that afternoon, the one thought that most touched me was his concluding evaluation of the whole experience. "I am convinced," Paul said very quietly, "that the main reason for fatherhood is to help us understand sonship."

Sonship? What does it mean to be truly a child of God? Is it not to have a striking family resemblance? Since the Father loves His creation to the point of total self-giving and the Son bears all human suffering, family membership surely must mean a willingness to carry other's burdens even when it is very painful. Motivating people through love accomplishes more than any amount of coercion. My friend Paul was changed from a disciplinarian into a disciple, from a drill sergeant into a devout son of the Father. Perhaps as at no other time in his life, Paul reflected the image of God during those moments of sitting in the corner.

Why is life so painful? Unless I have the capacity to hurt, I can't discover this principle of sonship. Hurting with people is infinitely more creative than imposing force. Growing up in a warped world makes all of us fearful that we have no other option but to resort to coercion and brawn. We develop behavior tendencies that are devious, self-righteous, and punitive. With time these patterns become like a mask that is hard, rigid, and emotionless, concealing the true face that is kind and caring. Unfortunately these masks generally don't get cracked and stripped away except through agonizing circumstances.

Here's another principle about how the image of God is realized in us. Being a servant is hard; being a suffering servant is doubly difficult. Yet taking on the pain of another person seems to put "God shoes" on our feet like nothing else. We start to look like the One we profess to believe in. Our flesh is peeled back and His goodness is revealed.

Does God know how great the hurt is? Most certainly, and He gives us the capacity to know and bear agony in the same way. In so doing, we are being given an extraordinary opportunity to be like our Father. The issue is not what we are, but what we are becoming.

THE IMAGE EXPRESSED

We hurt so much because we have such great potential.

When both the apostle Paul and Paul Cardin speak of sonship, they are expressing our extraordinary endowment.

Please understand that this biblical phrase has nothing to do with gender. Rather, the idea of sonship reflects an ancient period in history when the firstborn son inherited all that belonged to the father. Sonship implied relationship and privilege that is now available to all men and women. In addition, the concept reflects the incredible connectedness in the life and person of Jesus of Nazareth that completely reflected the love of the heavenly Father. The apostle Paul believed this bond was not singular, but a precedent for what was to happen in us.

Sonship is the title that describes our adoption into the family of God. More than carrying the family name, we are to look like one of the children. Paul wrote, "For those whom he foreknew he also predestined to be conformed to the image of His Son in order that He might be the first-born among many brethren."[2] Male or female, we are intended to become like Jesus. When people observe our actions, our caring, and our loving over the years, they should be able to see that we are coming more and more to look like our Elder Brother.

Even those who do not believe in Jesus Christ as a unique expression of God recognize that the world would be vastly improved if everybody were like Him. The idea alone challenges the imagination of the doubters. On the other hand, Christians are really excited by the suggestion that the sum total of their daily experience could cause them to become something like He was. Both the faithful and skeptics can conclude that implications of sonship raise enormous hopes and dreams in the human imagination.

Unfortunately so many only tack on the family name of Christian as if it were no more than a noun rather than an adjective that clearly defines identity. For those people the name Christian merely implies a belief system with no subsequent inner transformation. Far more, kinship means the reshaping of all that we are into all that Christ was. Tragically, many of us are only reflections of our society being styled by whatever is the current vogue in fashion, ideas, and commitment. This lack of metamorphosis is a serious issue not only for the church, but for individuals. Rather than the realization of potential, we tend to reflect the disintegration of culture.

Herein is the role of suffering. As painful reconstructive surgery can provide a new face, suffering can reshape our perspective, commitments, and dreams, breaking us free from cultural molds. Suffering has the power to twist, turn, try, and temper until the Christlike possibility comes forth. Every encounter with pain has in it the seeds of promise.

The apostle Peter came to a similar conclusion. He perceived that suffering is an arena in which our potential is finally and fully realized. In fact, he went further and stated that suffering can be viewed as part of the Divine program for personal fulfillment. "For to this you have been called, because Christ also suffered for you, leaving you an example that you should follow in his steps."[3] Humbly resisting our inclinations for revenge, retaliation, vindication, and exoneration is the opportunity where sonship is realized.

Whether you are fully in touch with it or not, you do have this potential.

CONCLUSIONS

Does God know how hard and dark and deep the hurt is? Yes, He does. His answer to us lies in the Cross of Jesus Christ where His Son died. Far from an incongruent, meaningless, unjust imposition on humanity, pain reflects how much we are like our heavenly Father. We can hurt so much because we have such great potential.

Therefore, we must not shrink from either the possibility of being hurt or from the work that it accomplishes. So here are some principles by which we can live:

- Because pain peels away the past, the issue is never what we are, but what we are becoming.
- When faced with abuse, betrayal, or injustice, the issue isn't the action taken against me; what counts is my reaction.
- Every encounter with pain has in it the seeds of promise.
- Those who stoop to be servants will rise to become sons.

Let's finish with the summation that Paul gave us

about the meaning of all our excruciating experiences. As one who had lived with great personal rejection, profound hardship, and would finally be put to death for his convictions, his insight is not to be discounted. He wrote, "I consider that the sufferings of this present time are not worth comparing with the glory that is to be revealed to us. For the creation waits with eager longing for the revealing of the sons of God."[4] His conclusion? The potential is worth the price.

GOING IN TO COME OUT

Often we have to go deeply into ourselves in order to be able to come out looking like God intended us to be. So what does the image of God look like in you? What sort of interior is exposed when you allow yourself to take on the servant role? Let's look.

Now you are ready to start a second section in your journal. Entitle this material, "Progressing." We are ready to understand how we might be actually developing during these difficult days. We will consider two more questions.

First, how am I discovering that I am stronger than I thought? What have my trials revealed about my ability to endure, to accept, and to remain faithful? What surprises have there been in how I have been able to handle what has happened? I want to look at my past performance to become aware of what I can build on in the future. What resources have I found in myself that I can remember to draw on?

Second, where am I weaker than I might have believed? Most of us practice an incredible amount of deception and denial. We will do almost anything to avoid seeing the painful parts of our past. If I refuse to deal with the debris of yesterday, it will eventually deal with me. Moreover, if I let the past sour in my soul, it will create an infection that will ultimately contaminate every area of my life. I have to become lucid about what I don't want to see. So this assignment is concerned with identifying what we consider to be our weaknesses. It isn't important what anyone else thinks about these qualities; the issue is how do I view these cracks in my foundation.

Once again you will want to summarize your findings after you have worked through the issues. Entitle these two columns, "Strengths" and "Weaknesses."

Obviously this reflection could take days, weeks, and even months to complete. Meanwhile, you will want to go ahead reading the book and following some of the other suggestions. In fact, later we will be building on this section. We are not in any hurry to wrap up these reflections. Depth, not speed, is our concern.

You may find yourself saying, "I'm not sure I've got the time for all of this work." Let me encourage you. There are key moments in our lives when the season is ripe and we *must* make time if we are going to heal the wounds of the past. If what I have described sounds like something that you ought to do, why not consider this as Divine intervention?

PART TWO

*Getting
Lost
in the
Dark*

WITHOUT
A
WHOLE
SOUL
IS THERE
ONLY
A
HOLE?

4

CAN I COME THROUGH PAIN TO PERSONHOOD?

"I want to concentrate on thanking you for this time in my life . . ." (Ps. 56).

If I told you my friend Nancy's screen name, chances are you might have seen one of her movies. For a period of time she was in high demand, but in recent years she has virtually disappeared from sight, like so many before her. In her youth she was a torrid portrayer of sensuality. Her private life was equally torrid. Nancy's endless sexual escapades led to chronic drug use, an illegitimate child, marital failure, disillusionment, and now obscurity and virtual poverty. Yet Nancy's most serious loss is her soul.

Nancy's former lifestyle is depicted in a new genre of literature. Purporting to describe the current generation, these books steam with the seamy side of life experienced by teens and young adults in the late eighties. *Slave of New York* and *Bright Lights, Big City* describe young people on drugs, living only for thrills. These youth have become no more than zombies.

Less than Zero is a book about young people in Beverly Hills who have everything money will buy. As one thumbs through these pages, the book reads like a contemporary packaging of the ancient story of the fall of the Roman Empire. Nevertheless, a very significant number of people are currently in pursuit of the very existence that has stripped Nancy and others like her of their dignity as human beings.

The sexual revolution of the sixties brought a new way of life to America, which was actually the reappearance of pagan hedonism. The pursuit of unbridled sensuality has become the preoccupation of a large segment of this society. Unrestrained physical pleasure is considered the ultimate good. Nancy is a prototype of this ideal. However, the debris of her life is its own commentary on the social upheaval.

Dr. Rollo May, a psychiatrist, has observed that the playboy philosophy has taken the fig leaf from the genitals and put it over the face. Certainly this is true in Nancy's case. Her unique personality and personhood have been obliterated. The only remaining aspect of her self that seems to be of worth is her body. However, Nancy has now discovered that swapping the body for the soul is a poor trade.

The movie actress, Carrie Fisher, has written a best seller, *Postcards from the Edge*. Her portrayal of one person's struggle to survive the drug culture highlights the national drug crisis where cocaine and chemical abuse has become a disastrous epidemic of monstrous proportions.

We know that addiction will kill body and soul. However, chemical abuse is often the consequence more than the cause.

The problem of inner deadness has often prompted the attempt to lose or find oneself in a drug-induced high. Our wide-spread social dependence on artificial stimulants has been created by a desperate and misguided search for anything that will fill the spiritual vacuum in empty lives.

Affluence, ease, conformity, emptiness, self-indulgence, self-serving, and self-centered preoccupation all combine to produce a banal, bland, passionless, colorless world. Faceless people who live in vast wastelands of subways, crammed freeways, jammed airports, and lonely apartments will quickly opt for any form of sensuality that has the feel of life. However, trading bodies, pills, booze, cocaine, money, and power for the soul results in sensual suicide.

How big a problem are we facing? Every year thirty-eight million prescriptions are filled for Valium, forty-five million for sleeping pills, and nearly thirteen million for barbiturates. The meaning of this data is hard to assess since the order may range from fifty to one hundred or more pills each time.[1] No statistics are available on illegal usage. However, estimates indicate nineteen million sleeping pills are taken each night and seventeen billion aspirin are consumed each year. But when the soul leaves, you cannot take enough pills to fill up the hole.

Of course, most of us don't live in the exotic world of Nancy and Carrie. Nevertheless, I see people every week whose lives differ only in degree. The answer to many of their broken marriages, dissolved dreams, and resultant loss of self worth is actually spiritual in nature.

When I encounter people caught in the confusion of these situations, I ask them to step back and take a second look at the nature of the brokenness in which they seem trapped. Is there any spark of the Divine left? Is there any meaning to their pursuits? Any dreams left they can recapture? To lose all sense of God is finally to lose everything else. These people are committing sensual suicide. They have lost their souls.

FROM PAIN TO PERSONHOOD

I have reluctantly, but finally, come to the conclusion that suffering will always be part of human experience because of its indispensable role in the recovery of the soul.

Pain is not to be avoided but lived through. The value of suffering is that as it is endured, the condition may not be corrected, but the person will be transformed. Far more important than getting off the hook is the aging, maturing, curing, and remolding that ultimately result in either a new or an improved humanity. Psychoanalyst Carl Jung once observed that in the successful treatment of neurosis, the condition is not corrected as much as the person learns to handle the problem more appropriately. The same thing happens when we inquire about how pain affects the discovery of our soul. These encounters with suffering are resolved not through relief but resurrection.

We must carefully explore what it means to salvage

our soul and the part that trauma plays in the restoration. In the subsequent two chapters, we will explore this theme looking at the biblical perspective and a personal reflection on how the soul is recovered through suffering. Paul's suggestion that we can "be conformed to the image of God's Son" has vast implications. Since God is working in everything for good, we can know that the end result is to become a person with a soul like the one seen in Jesus of Nazareth. If such is possible, then pain is indeed gain.

But first we must carefully explore the meaning of such a loss in ourselves. Let me pose a haunting question. Could you lose your soul and not even know it's gone? Could suffering be your last opportunity to save yourself? Is it possible to have a form of spiritual cancer working within that has been eating up the true us, without our even being aware? Some readers may discover they have mistaken the cancer itself for their soul. Sound a little scary? It should.

SEEING WHAT ISN'T THERE

One of Jesus' most cryptic warnings was that it is possible to win the world and lose one's soul. The implication is clear. We can be so busy surveying our gains that we lose the capacity to recognize that our very essence has evaporated. Unless we recover the ability to see what is no longer there, we may be so satisfied with our accomplishments and accumulations that we miss the fact that the best part of us is missing. So how shall we become aware?

First, we need to have some idea of the meaning and place of soul. I will start with the image that I find conveyed in the words and works of Jesus of Nazareth as we develop a biblical definition.

Jesus was uniquely aware of what the soul is and how it is nurtured. He was able to fully and completely enjoy and communicate with others, himself, nature, and His Father. His capacity to live with purpose and joy reveals the soul. In contrast, the loss of ability to relate in any of these areas constitutes the loss of soul. In this sense, recovery of affection can be one way to reconstitute the soul. In a word, the soul is the place of ultimate related-ness and connection.

Moreover, our human uniqueness is carried in the soul. When we lose touch with our promise, we become a caricature of our true selves and begin to function ac-cording to the images that we try to sell to the public. We may simply shrivel into a flat, hollow shell or inflate into a bag of empty hot air. The soul is the bearer or container of our authenticity.

Explaining the loss of soul is relatively difficult since we are not dealing with the absence of a body part, but the subtraction of being itself. Loss of connection and genuineness generally happens slowly and by degree. The problem is much like trying to explain to a child or a primitive person the meaning of oxygen. Breathing is so natural and the atmosphere so transparent that the air can't be appreciated until it begins to be diminished. The discomfort actually helps us label and identify what's missing. Often our anxiety, anguish, and emo-tional pain are clues that our soul is sick or being con-sumed.

Should the internal signs be ignored or discounted long enough, we will eventually reach that place of lost-ness of which Jesus warned us. We need soul-stirring pain as a flashing red light signaling impending disaster in our inner world.

Much of our spiritual pain is the soul's attempt to make us realize that it is being starved and that what is slipping away is of extreme value.

In the beginning, we may not have any idea of the value of the message. In fact, we will probably despise what seems to be bubbling up within us and assume that it surely must be evil. While such pain can have a physi-cal or psychological component, it is still symptomatic of a deeper, more spiritual cause. The soul may actually be generating internal pressure, trying to bring us to con-sciousness with a completely new and more eternal per-spective. These times of transition may well appear as the 3:00 A.M. agony when the night becomes unbearably long.

In order to bring "what isn't there" into focus, I want to tell you about a number of case studies of people with whom I have either worked or have a first-hand acquaintance. As I do so, I will tell you how similar situations are reflected in literature. At each point, although the heart wasn't close to quitting, suffering was a warning that spiritual death was occurring.

DEADLY DETACHMENT

Indifference and insensitivity kill the soul. Aloofness eventually becomes a deadly form of aloneness. With that fact in mind let me introduce you to Larry. I have known him for many years extending through my service to a number of parishes. While I tried many times to help him with his problems, my attempts were futile. His suspicion and resistance to change made it impossible for anyone to crack through, to help him get in touch with the world that existed beyond his own selfish needs. As I watched him become an old man, I saw his soul turn to stone.

Interestingly enough, Larry always had some interest in religious things and often talked with me about church matters. However, in every conversation he clearly kept himself at a distance both from God and from the pain of other people. He actually used churchly matters as his final line of defense against a real and deep encounter with the Holy Spirit. Always an observer, Larry could never let himself be a full participant.

Larry has not been able to sustain a meaningful relationship with women because he does not know how to give. He has treated women as momentary distractions or diversions when his aloneness turned into boredom. His inability to care has consigned him to a solitary existence, as if he were locked in a cell in some forlorn institution.

Pain? Larry's life has been increasingly filled with it.

Never allowing any difficulty to soften him, each tinge of loneliness has turned into cynicism and despair. As Larry's life slips away each day, more and more of his uniqueness and personhood also vanish.

When I think about Larry, I am often reminded of some of the characters in James Joyce's masterpiece, *The Dubliners*. His tales of the hollow existence of the people who lived in Dublin at the turn of the last century depict the slow but steady death of the soul. In *A Painful Case*, Joyce describes the inner life of James Duffy and exposes the emptiness of a man who lived for nothing but the repetition of a proper but emotionally void existence. Like Larry, James lived only for himself and his moral rectitude.

James's routine was broken once when he happened upon Emily Sinico. In a rare moment of self-revelation, he touched her affections. Moved by the neediness of his life, she suddenly took his hand and pressed it to her cheek. Such an overt display of passion had surprised and offended his sensitivities. Shortly thereafter he told Emily that they must end their relationship. Seeing how upset she was, he left quickly.

Two years later he noticed an article in the paper about the untimely death of a lady who seemed to have stepped in front of a train. The article noted that a woman named Emily Sinico had been despondent for two years and may have been drunk when she died. The paper referred to her death as "a painful case." At first Duffy resisted recognizing the implications that were so clearly in the story, but slowly, painfully, he faced the truth.

He might have saved her life. Now Emily Sinico was nothing more than a quickly vanishing memory. The thought made James Duffy feel overwhelmingly alone, and made him recognize fully her aloneness and how he could have filled her life with some meaning. But he hadn't. Now James knew the truth. He had sentenced her to death. And in so doing, he had consigned himself to being no more than another passing memory that would soon also disappear without meaning and purpose. He, too, would fade as only another "painful case."

Larry and James lost their souls. Their loneliness went unnoticed and unobserved. Rather than reach out for the warmth of love that comes from giving ourselves away, they had settled for a void in which they barely existed. In denying their pain, they had ignored the means of salvation.

We are meant to live with passion even when it is painful. Joyce explores this theme in his final short story that became the award winning film, *The Dead*. During a turn of the century Christmas party in Dublin, we meet a cast of characters who have lost their zest for life and now can only go through the motions of a celebration which is no more than a ritual. As the evening ends, Gabriel realizes how life has slipped by them and he sees the flatness of his own existence. He muses that it is better to "pass boldly into that other world, in the full glory of some passion, than fade and wither dismally with age."

Tearfully Gabriel recognizes that he has never passionately loved anyone and that "his own identity is fading out into a gray unpalatable world."

On behalf of these three lost souls, take a second look in your mirror. Unless we love and share, we become no more than locusts who are sustained by what they devour. Certainly loved ones die and their absence causes great pain. Yet without relatedness and its possibilities for grief, we can never know fullness of joy.

WHEN SOCIETY STRANGLES

As we can gain the world and lose our souls, so can society conquer and devour us. Governments, political ideologies, societies, local communities, and pressure groups have the power to consume us and turn us into mere fleeting shadows on the passing scene.

Such imagery brings a cast of characters before my eyes. At once I think of Melvin Longfoot, a Cheyenne Indian with whom I went to high school. The demeaning, insensitive environment which surrounded us sent him into alcoholism and an early death. Then there is Buzz, whose inner world was destroyed in the jungles of Vietnam. Much like the hero in the movie *Coming Home*, Buzz never was really able to come back because the brutality of war killed something precious in his spirit. I've seen the same haunted vacancy in the eyes of people all over the world. Society can truly shred our spirituality.

Occasionally I wonder what has become of Llyin, whom I met in the Soviet Union. He had traveled with us for several days before we found out why he was a part of our group. One afternoon he confided that he was a professional propagandist for the Communist Party and that he was accompanying our group, trying to understand how we functioned. He had concluded that Christians produced better propaganda than Communists, and he was interested in learning our techniques. Obviously we were rather shocked by his explanation.

"Why would you think we are better at telling our story?" I asked.

"Because today in the Soviet Union," he replied in excellent English, "we have more youth turning to the church than joining the Party."

"Really!"

"Surely the only reason," Llyin continued, "is because of propaganda."

We tried to explain that maybe there was a spiritual reality drawing young people to the Christian faith that had nothing to do with manipulating facts and ideas. Such a possibility was inconceivable to our traveling companion. Llyin had been taught to be an atheist and had joined the Communist Party in college as a good career choice. He ended the conversation by saying, "You see, I do not believe in the soul. When you are dead, you are just dead."

We know a great deal about what produces Llyin's mentality. The possibility of faith was strangled. No one has chronicled the process better than Aleksandr Solzhenitsyn. His *One Day in the Life of Ivan Denisovich* and the "Gulag" stories are the result of his nearly fifty years of studying the Russian Revolution. The destruction of churches, the imprisonment and deaths of tens of thousands of church leaders, and the militant assault of Marxist atheism on faith is now common history. However, the jolting surprise for us is what Solzhenitsyn concluded during his exile in the Western world.

In his now famous graduation address to Harvard University, Solzhenitsyn turned his eye to the American scene and issued the warning that life here may be more disastrous to the soul than in the Soviet Union. He pointed to our luxury-ridden society as a place where one is more apt to be swallowed by the comfortable than in a state where persecution makes for a tough and resilient spirit. In the tones of an Old Testament prophet, he preached to the college graduates that unless they recovered an experience of God, they would be in far worse shape than their Soviet counterparts. He warned that the continual siphoning away of spiritual strength by the process of secularization was a far greater danger than external attacks on religion. When the meaning of life is reduced to nothing higher than the pursuit of happiness, then all hope is lost. Such are the insights of a man who through extraordinary suffering has developed a great and expansive soul.

Two contrasting images immediately leap into my mind: one of an expansive soul, the other of withered and distorted souls. The first is the face of a Russian Orthodox priest, Father Boris, whom I traveled with from Moscow to the monastery of St. Vladimir in Zagorsk. Trained in the Soviet system to be a scientist, he had turned his back on a secure life to become a priest of the church. We talked of how he had been raised on a traditional diet of atheistic teaching. Yet as he considered the suffering he saw in the world around him, he could not live with materialistic rational answers to his eternal questions. His quest for answers to cruelty he had witnessed during and following World War II had brought him to the conviction that he did have a soul. In turn God found him.

I see another image in sharp contrast to the world of Father Boris and Aleksandr Solzhenitsyn. The recent fad of the *Donahue, Geraldo,* and *Oprah* talk shows has found the most embarrassing, scandalous examples of personal immorality and put them on the screen for the world to watch as they air their dirty laundry. Apparently the hosts, having run out of anything intelligent to say, are left with only the banal and the anal. On one particular afternoon Geraldo was interviewing three women whose lives had been linked to national scandal. Loudly and explicitly they shared their sexual secrets. One of the women, a former stripper, was claiming to have had sex with everybody from a president to Elvis Presley. I wondered if these people had mothers, fathers, children, or even grandchildren who might have to hear these recitations of their degrading demonstrations of low self-worth and self-esteem. In contrast to the Orthodox priest and the author who had paid such a great price for the recovery of their souls, these women were exposing their emptiness and deadness to the world as entertainment.

And what about us? If we can step back a moment from the sensational, we need ponder our own personal horizons and ask ourselves to what degree has our environment mangled and mutilated the sensitivities on which our souls feed.

Research tells us that the average American young adult will see fifty thousand murders or attempted murders on the television screen by the time he or she is eighteen.[2] The average fourteen-year-old will see more than thirteen thousand deaths. The typical five-year-old will observe more than two hundred hours of similar violence.[3] In a typical evening more gunshots are fired on television than in one year in a medium-sized American city.[4]

Where's the supervision to monitor these soul-devouring scenes that are entering young minds? Comparable studies have found that the contemporary business executive spends about five minutes a day on the average with his or her children.

The lack of a positive role model creates a vacuum on two fronts. As these children become adults, the record for personal concern in too many cases reflects what the desensitization of television violence has done to them. The stories of mugging, rape, and assault victims who lay helplessly crying out to ignoring passersby for help is jolting. Many homes in our major cities are literally fortresses to protect them from criminals on the streets and to sequester them from what is transpiring on the pavement.

Remember our issue is what has happened to our souls. What has happened to us in a world of violence and indifference? Rather than tragedy awakening us to pain and need, we lose the very sensitivity so essential to making us human.

Suffering is turned into a spectator sport.

THROUGH PAIN TO PROMISE

Now do you see the meaning of the loss of the soul? And where are you when you look inward? Perhaps the necessity of struggle in the process of recovery has become much clearer. Our dark nights can become the most important times of our life even though years may pass before we are fully aware of the meaning of these confusing times of transition. Without suffering, there would not be transformation. "If it were not for our unique wounds, we would not have our unique gifts." Pain has its place.

Through these stories and personal experiences, we can see that the heavenly Father often uses suffering the way a surgeon uses the finest knife to cut away and remove obstacles to the healing of the whole person.

I am not suggesting that God visits tragedy upon us for our well-being. However, it is clear that He is most able to use what may not have been intended, turning our disasters into extraordinary opportunities for growth. When we reflect on these times of disappointment and trial, the experiences can become like a probe, a retractor, or a scalpel opening us up through spiritual surgery to redemptive possibilities. Loneliness may be necessary.

Sometimes a prescription for solitude may seem worse than the performance of a multitude of back-breaking tasks. Nevertheless, we seldom find ourselves while we're waiting in the 5:00 P.M. rush hour traffic in a subway; nor is the reality of God found in the midst of a freeway. More likely places for us to find our way through confusion and conflict are in the solitude of quiet forests and dim sanctuaries, the hush that falls with sunsets over farm ponds, and the gentle sound of rain on window panes when we're alone. Unfortunately, most of us will do almost anything to avoid the deafening sound of such silence. We keep our televisions going full tilt, our stereos up to a few decibels below the pain threshold, and our schedules too full to allow personal confrontation time. The solitude that is necessary to discover the full truth about ourselves can be more ominous than any trip to the hospital. Perhaps the middle of the night is the only time left for necessary reflections.

Facing the truth about our fear, anxiety, and guilt can be so overwhelming, we become convinced we will not survive the confrontation. Yet we will—and in the process find release. We may discover patterns in our personalities that are destructive to others and that destroy our best relationships. Owning up to the corrections that require fundamental change in the very structure of our identity is usually of staggering proportions. Again, the travail is the price of a new birth.

Every day hundreds of people face the truth about their addictions for the first time. Confessing failure to control one's life is humiliating. Nevertheless, recovery is possible only when we choose to recognize the message that pain has been sending us. In all of these incidents, as well as many more, the only way our souls will be found is by going through pain—rather than avoiding it.

I find in a story from Peter Dimitri a parable about each of our lives.

Huge slides were constructed on the river banks of a

great forest for sending logs down smooth troughs into the river to be floated down to the sawmill. At end of day, lumberjacks would slide down the chutes sitting on their axe handles. Late one afternoon while making his descent, a lumberjack caught his leg in one of the joints in the ramp. At the same moment someone at the top decided to send one last tree to the river. Without warning an enormous log was pushed at the top into the chute. Unable to pry his leg loose, the terrified logger looked up to see certain death bearing down upon him. He had only a moment in which to make a decision. The issue was simple; either he would lose his leg or his life. Quickly raising his ax, the forester hacked off his leg and fell free to the ground.

Dimitri concludes this story with the cryptic comment, "He was crippled for life, but at least he was alive!"[5]

CONCLUSION

We can lose what we were not aware we had. Each of us must carefully examine our inner world for evidence of a hole where there should be a soul. Suffering is often our only hope for recovery and salvation.

- In accumulating everything, we can end up with nothing.
- Radical surgery may be required for survival.
- Our pain can restore our personhood.

We must be prepared to cut.

THE
HOLE
THAT WAS
YOUR
SOUL
CAN STILL
MAKE
YOU
WHOLE

5

WHERE IS MY CENTER AND MY CIRCUMFERENCE?

"Because you have already delivered me . . ." (Ps. 56).

In Chaim Potok's *The Chosen,* two Jewish boys search for their destinies and their souls. Reuven is the son of a conservative Jewish scholar, while Daniel Saunders is the brilliant and gifted son of the Rebbe of a community of Hassidic Jews. The story revolves around the strange family relationship of Reb Saunders and Daniel. The Rebbe never speaks directly to his son. Soon Reuven recognizes how much pain the silence has caused his friend. In time, Reuven becomes a trusted friend of both father and son. Finally he learns the secret of the shunning when the Rebbe explains himself to both boys.

While Daniel is treated almost as an eavesdropper, the Rebbe recounts to Reuven the remarkable childhood of his son who at four years of age could not only read stories in Yiddish, but could recount a story from memory with every detail perfectly in place. However, the astonished father soon realized that this dazzling child lacked compassion and sympathy. The Rebbe was frightened at the arrogance and indifference of a boy who could only rejoice in his remarkable mind and in excelling over others. He was terrified by the evil potential of such a child.

When Rebbe Saunders pondered what to do, he remembered one of the ways that his own father had taught him—silence. By forcing him to walk around within himself, Reb Saunders' father caused him to become acquainted with his own heart and soul. Inner strength had surfaced. Reflecting on this, the Rebbe decided that he must raise his own son in such a manner. He concluded that only the pain of prolonged silence could save his son from arrogance.

As Daniel listened, he learned for the first time why his father had appeared to shun him.

> One learns of the pain of others by suffering one's own pain, by turning inside oneself, by finding one's own soul. And it is important to know of pain. It destroys our self-pride, our arrogance, our indifference toward others. It makes us aware of how frail and tiny we are and of how much we must depend upon the Master of the Universe.[1]

With tears streaming down his face, Daniel realized for the first time the profound love that his father had for him. Enduring the loss of relationship that he might have enjoyed with his son, the father himself had paid a great price. Nevertheless, recovery of the boy's soul was critical. And pain was the means of restoration.

What motivated the Rebbe? What was he seeking to awaken when he pushed his son into silence? From his studies of the Torah, he had learned something of great significance. He knew both the meaning of the soul and the place of tribulation required for its recovery.

THE SHAPE OF WHOLENESS

While Hassidics like Reb Saunders tend to be a mystery to most in both religious and secular worlds, they are people of faith who have pursued questions about the soul and have often been more concerned with the answers than many other religious communities. They have found the Old Testament an ideal place to start in the quest to understand the soul. The history of the Jewish people is the story of a suffering servant-people who, through their pain, have sought to help the world find its own soul. In many ways the nation of Israel was *prima facie* evidence of the value and need for suffering in bringing redemption.

We can find important clues in the Bible in our quest for our own soul and the meaning of our struggles. In this chapter we will seek to understand further the meaning of the soul by exploring the Scriptures. If suffering is going to help us become complete, we must know what wholeness looks like. So what does Scripture mean by the soul?

WHAT IS THE SOUL?

The soul is the true me. Psychology uses the question, "Who am I?" to define our uniqueness. While I may generally define my personhood from the sum total of my experiences, biblically the soul means that I have an additional transcendent component. However, the Bible extends all human definitions, encompassing them with an eternal identity. Psychology explains what my environment has given me. The soul defines what God put in me from the beginning.[2]

However, before I can fully grasp the biblical perspective of the *soul*, I must define two other words: *heart* and *spirit*. The mishmash of the modern usage of these words lacks the precision to give us real insight. Still, each of these concepts must be clear before we can understand what Scripture means by the soul. To add to the confusion, the Bible sees us as a unit in which each of these parts is a piece of the whole. The heart, spirit, and soul are distinctly different concepts although the soul encompasses both heart and spirit. The Bible speaks of that final singleness as our soul.

In order to understand the unity which our soul brings to us, we must start by going back and looking at all of the pieces. We will examine these components somewhat in the same order in which we become aware of their existence in us. Since our feelings are the beginning point, let's see what the Bible means by the heart.

Have a Heart

Can you remember a Christmas in your childhood that was particularly happy and exciting for you? Think about that day for a moment and let the scenes of the lights, the tree, and all the presents drift before your eyes. Linger in the glow and excitement, and see if you can remember any special gift you received and why that was such a wonderful time for you. When you are in touch with those memories, affections, and the warmth, you will have found your heart.

The Bible indicates that our impressions and emotional experiences are kept there. Memories and rules are stored in this invisible place. The heart is the sorting room where we put labels and interpretations on past events. This inner spiritual zone is the seat of our emotions. Pain lives on in the heart.[3]

As children, we become aware of the heart before we recognize the other components that make a spiritual journey possible. Initially I am concerned with little more than how experiences "feel" to me. In fact, most of us have far more sensitivity than we are aware of because emotions from our childhood may be so powerful that, in order to endure the intensity, we learn to shut them down. However, if we are going to really come to know our soul, we will have to endure some of that suffering again in order to become fully aware of all the dimensions of this house in which the soul resides.

The Bible describes the heart not only as a place of receiving but also as a center of giving out. My experiences, values, and feelings come together in my heart and merge into responses and plans of action. The heart turns my impressions into deeds. Like a fountain, these reactions pour forth from the heart.[4]

For example, I remember quite vividly the first time that I was fully aware of my wife. I had reached the statesman age of sixteen and she was all of fifteen. Various impressions, thoughts, attractions, and wants had been gurgling around in my head since I had found out who she was several months earlier. The moment of awakening came at a friend's party. I was seated at the bottom of the stairs when she descended; she looked extraordinarily fetching. Deep down inside a thought came bubbling up shouting, *Go for it!* My emotions were being turned into action. At that moment I truly knew that I had a heart.

The heart also attaches value to our experiences. What the Bible means by the heart is certainly more profound than what psychology means by emotions. More than just feelings, the heart attributes purpose and worth to events. The writers of Scripture recognize that our feelings can't really be separated from their meaning without losing their significance. Without the work of the heart, my suffering is no more than bad sensations running through my nervous system.[5]

The heart is able to take tragic moments of injustice and find a more hope-filled interpretation to make these traumas bearable. If I can find a constructive place for undeserved times that I must live through, the pain can be transformed. So the heart is potentially a divine filtration system that can purify the dirty experiences until they have a constructive place in my memory.

Dr. Victor Frankl was one of the first psychiatrists to recognize the extraordinary capacity we have to bear suffering and give meaning to tragedy. A Jewish survivor of the Nazi death camps, Dr. Frankl found he was able to bear the terrible conditions of brutality by focusing his mind on memories filled with love. Later he discovered he could help many distraught clients by leading them to realize the purpose in their tribulations. His observations confirm the place of the heart in helping us overcome our own suffering.

So the heart is the natural starting place in our search for the soul. Perhaps it would seem that our feelings ought to bring us rather quickly to our souls. However, our emotions are often the most unreliable test of reality that we have. The Bible cautions that the heart can be deceitful and filled with evil intent. Moreover, Scripture warns that the heart can become hard, fat, and corrupted.[6] Such concrete language depicts the fact that our emotions can become so distorted that they cease to be accurate barometers or moral compasses. Thus, rather than taking us to our soul, our feelings can actually become a deterrent. The fact that I feel is neither an indication that my perception is correct nor that something eternal is working in me. I must not mistake my emotions for my soul.

Affliction sometimes distorts our emotional reality. Abuse from childhood will certainly color our perceptions. Generally our feelings need a lot of healing. What can we do if we suspect that we have distorted emotions? We may need to have our feeling life revitalized before we can begin to find our way to the soul.

The Christian community has discovered that rejuvenation occurs as the Holy Spirit touches individual lives. When you seek the reality of the risen Christ to enter your heart, you open yourself up to revitalization of the heart.

Some of us need the help of a professional counselor or a pastor to fully realize the new freedom that God is waiting to give us through this "open heart surgery" that He alone performs from within. Don't be afraid to seek the help you may need. The renewal of the heart is the beginning point in finding eternal identity and destiny.

Repeatedly as people surrender their inner pain to God through prayer, they experience surprising peace that seems to arise from within. While circumstances have not changed, they have an inner tranquility that sustains them. Harmony and calmness have come to their hearts. This process of receiving the Holy Spirit is the beginning of the restoration of their soul.

The Inner Force

The next step in our mental development is the emergence of the spirit. Spirit is the Bible's term for the motivating force in our personality. Somewhere in our earliest years, people begin to recognize that there is a distinct quality to each personality. The Bible calls this sparkle a spirit. Some people may be described as high-spirited or full of spirit; other people will be labeled as docile or having a lack of spirit. The temper of our spirit is generally expressed in our will power. In time we become aware of how the spirit is different from the heart.[7]

Our oldest sons are eleven months apart in age with the oldest having always been the physically smaller of the two. From birth, Todd had the typical spirit of the first-born; he was always assertive. He loved contact sports and made quite a wrestler. Tony was a more gentle, sensitive child who loved reading and, predictably, became a writer. While modern psychology might describe their differences in terms of aptitudes and personality structure, the Bible would have simply said that one had the spirit of a warrior and the other the spirit of a poet.

Many years had to pass before we could say with any accuracy that one did have the soul of a fighter and the other the soul of a bard. When little warriors grow up, tame their tempers, and turn out to have the souls of lovers, we are often surprised by how the soul was different from what the spirit seemed to be.

We need to make sure we understand the biblical meaning of spirit, lest we also confuse being spirited as being the same as expressing our soul. The Bible proclaims that we can be filled with God's Spirit. However, these exhilarating moments are not necessarily the same as an encounter with our soul. Yet, the encounter with the Holy Spirit is a prerequisite for the realization of our soul.

As the Spirit of God invades our inner world, this presence becomes a part of our spirit. When this intermingling happens, a vital ingredient is added to our capacity to function effectively.

The Bible promises two important results can follow. First, the Spirit will empower us. Vitality and incentive are supplied by the Spirit. Second, creative energy results. These two dimensions of inner capacity can make an incredible difference in how we are able to face life.[8]

The Bible has many exciting descriptions of how various people were filled with the Spirit of God. New encouragement and zest gave these people a fresh drive to overcome what formerly defeated them. The empowering of the Spirit was much like finding new enthusiasm.

However, enthusiastic people certainly don't necessarily demonstrate the recovery of their souls. Motivational speeches, pep rallies, and political conventions are not the biblical equivalent of Moses on Mount Horeb, Jesus in Gethsemane, or Paul on the road to Damascus.

In the first chapter of the book of Haggai, we have a story about when the Spirit of God touched His people, immediately after Israel's exile. The Babylonians had smashed the nation and taken all of the political leadership into exile. Times were hard and money was scarce. To return from the flourishing country of Babylonia to the charred, pillaged remains of Jerusalem would take great courage. Hope was in short supply. Then Haggai recounts:

> And the LORD stirred up the spirit of Zerubbabel, the son of She-alti-el, governor of Judah, and the spirit of Joshua the son of Jehozadak, the high priest, and the spirit of all the remnant of the people; and they came and worked on the house of the LORD of hosts, their God.[9]

Their fear, doubt, and skepticism were overcome because a new spirit had filled them.

In our own quest for adequacy in the face of great difficulty, we often need to seek similar help. Such was the case with Margaret Williams. For months she and I had prayed about the impending death of her husband, George. Before being struck by cancer, he had been a vital and brilliant accountant. However, as the final stages of the rampaging disease took his strength, we struggled with the inevitability of his approaching death. Many people feared that Margaret would crumble and fall under the weight of caring for her children, facing the many uncertainties, and handling the loss of the man to whom she was devoted. In the hospital room we closed the final chapter of his life on earth by fervently praying together. Before my eyes I watched a new and powerful force take hold of her life. Far from crumbling, she became a pillar of support for everyone else. The strength and determination that carried her through the funeral into a new way of life left its mark on the community. She has been spiritually equipped to make a new and creative approach to life.

As the emergence of a definite spirit is part of the development of a child's personality, so the empowering of the Spirit is the next step in the development of our soul. Realizing that God's Spirit is working starts our recognition of what the soul means. We know that we can be more than we are and that our future is safe in God's hands. We realize that an adventure with the Divine is not reserved for mystics, prophets, preachers, and saints of the past. We sense that we, too, are made for an authentic, full relationship with our heavenly Father. Seeking to be filled with the Holy Spirit is the next step in the discovery of our soul.

Meet the Soul

Unfortunately, having heart, spirit, and a vivacious personality doesn't necessarily equate with having a vibrant soul. By the time we are six years old we know our emotions and have inner motivation, but we may be quite old before we become fully aware of either the presence or absence of our soul. The drive to succeed, the excitement of new adventure, or the sheer force of overwhelming sensuality may keep us functioning at such a clip that we are unaware of the shallowness of our life, the emptiness of our values, or the hollowness of personal meaning. Generally it takes pain to shake us into the knowledge that all of the inner lights aren't on. The development of our soul is not a matter of age but of sensitivity.

From the biblical point of view, the soul is the real us, our essence. When we speak of the unique creation of God that makes us eternally different from anything that has ever come into the world, we are talking about our soul. The soul represents the fingerprint of God on our lives. It is both the center and circumference of our existence.[10]

Without the encirclement of the soul, emotion and spirit become displaced, defused, and dissipated. The soul is the context in which the heart and spirit are intended to do their work. The older we become the more aware we are of how vital it is to have such a center. Unless life circulates around some core of meaning, in time it will become unbearable. Soap operas become nauseating and their plots disgusting because we can only stand so much gushy passion, artificial emotion, narcissistic preoccupation, and manufactured motivation before boredom sets in. While many people live and die without penetrating the surface of life, we are made for more.

When faced with issues that really matter, we come to life. For this reason pain and suffering have the potential to move us toward far greater dimensions within ourselves than we ever guessed existed.

Consequently the soul is the place where sorrow strikes. When Jesus wrestled in agony in the Garden of Gethsemane, He cried out, "My soul is very sorrowful even to death." Truly, grief can make us sick to the point of virtual demise. At the same time, death and despondency cause us to live out of our soul and put us in touch with our very essence. Nothing exposes the soul like pain.

The soul is not a place in us, nor is it an amorphous entity that "goes to heaven" when all the rest of us dies. The idea of a soul (psyche) that survives and floats away is the Greek idea that Plato expounded.

Rather than some indefinable carrier of vitality, the Bible indicates the soul is the true and total "us" that survives death when it has been touched by the life of God. However, when the soul is infected with death, it dies. As we are invaded by God's power, the "what-we-have-become" receives the promise of survival beyond this planet. So, biblically speaking, the soul describes the unity and totality of our life that is built for eternity.[11]

Although Plato taught that there is no sharp line between body and soul, the Bible makes an important distinction between the two.[12] Bodies are important, but the soul is far more significant than our physical condition. A vital soul endures and overcomes the limitations of the body.

As I write these words, the face of "Mamma Jane"

Dameron appears in my mind. This gracious, kind, elderly woman had an extraordinary presence that came from a full and well-developed soul. I first began to realize her depth when she told me that frequently, as she prepared in prayer for Sunday worship the night before, the exact text that I was about to preach came to her mind. Often I would receive her notes in the mail telling me of how she had felt a prompting to pray for me, though I had told no one of my need. Her messages of encouragement were of profound significance to me.

In her final years I often prayed for her physical needs; the inevitable grind of time took its toll. However, as her body wore out, the deterioration seemed only to expand Mamma Jane's soul.

I would call her at the nursing home and inquire about her well-being. The frail, little voice would tremble a bit but respond, "Oh, Robert, I am having the most glorious experiences. My joy is sublime."

"Oh," I would hesitate because her daughter had just told me how bad her condition was. "You are feeling okay?"

"I'm having these marvelous times in prayer. God has never been so real to me. He is right here!"

"But I thought you were experiencing a lot of pain."

"Well, yes, Robert. I can't walk any more and my heart's about to give out, but we all have our little problems."

And then Mamma Jane would enthusiastically tell me about her latest spiritual breakthrough. The fullness of her life blossomed as the outer husks of her physical body withered away.

When you consult Scripture about the realization of the soul, it points you to a cast of characters who had many of the same qualities I found in Mamma Jane. Look at Moses who was chased from the palace of the Pharaoh into the desert where he was stripped of all pride. When he finally came to the burning bush, Moses, having found his soul, could hear God speak. Consider the shepherd boy David, who sat peacefully among the sheep, listening to God speak in the wind, the lightning, and thunder, as well as in the absolute stillness of a magnificent spring day. Remember Samson, whose blunders and arrogance finally cost him his eyesight and his life. In darkness, pushing the grinding wheel like an animal, once more he found the presence of God and the ability to lay down his life for the good of his people.

The supreme picture of the fully developed soul was painted on Good Friday when Jesus looked down upon his tormentors and prayed, "Father, forgive them for they know not what they do." As these heroes of faith were endowed, so are we.

CONSEQUENTLY

We can *exist* with little or no knowledge of the "true us"; babies have no such awareness, and tragically, many people in mid-life and beyond are still in inner infancy. But this is not a fulfilling existence. Though their outward lives may appear prosperous, adult children's condition is reflected in the lack of unity within themselves. They have no sense of wholeness or completeness. Inner fragmentation follows.

Secular psychologist Dr. Carl Jung profoundly understood that many forms of emotional illness are essentially the result of a lost soul. While I don't agree with many of Jung's religious ideas, he is helpful because he talked about the soul from a scientific point of view. He recognized that what we call neurosis is fundamentally an inner state of war resulting from divisions in our soul. He observed that these conflicts begin as we develop two personalities that are in opposition to each other. In the words of Faust, "Two souls, alas, dwell in my breast apart." Only a spiritual reunion can end this civil war. Jung found that we must integrate our experiences in life—without apology or retreat—with the essence which God has given us. His exact prescription was to discover what Jesus meant when he said we must lose our life in order to find it. Jung saw little hope for recovery apart from a genuine religious experience.[13] Suffering is our internal warning system signaling a problem.

Much of the discomfort with which we struggle in the middle of the night is secondary. We may be wrestling with a broken marriage, business problems, or childhood fears, but the primary problem is our personal lostness. While we may find temporary succor if these symptoms are relieved, the pain will only come back in other forms until we have dealt with the displacement of the soul. Our inner confusion seeps and leaks out in many ways and forms.

Set adrift, people cannot have the awareness of creation that is necessary for a sense of well-being. Solidarity with all of God's creation and creatures is lost. Relationships with other people turn into nothing more than mechanical procedures for getting through twenty-four hours a day. We exist as no more than the sum total of our pursuits, wants, fears, ambitions, and drives. The speed with which we live creates such constant movement that we end up thinking that the push and the pace is life. Sunsets, sunrises, babies, balloons, puppies, and parades blur together in a meaningless smear of grayness as they whirl by unobserved and without meaning.

Of course, God is gone. There is no awareness of Presence at one's elbow. Without a sense of living life before God, we are preoccupied only with the physical realm. The health of the body is assumed to be a comment on the state of the soul. We become no more than the sum total of the roles that we play, the relationships we have, and the social masks that we wear. Warning! The Bible describes such an existence as "life in the flesh," which ends in death. We mistake activity for life, business for vitality, and sensation for soul. Eventually, life without God will come to feel like living death. In time the emptiness will kill us.

RESTORATION

But the biblical message is one of hope. We can recover what we didn't know we had lost. Let's look at the promise. Our scriptural explorations have given us some important clues about the unique characteristics of those who have recovered their soul. Having become aware of their own uniqueness, they have found their special place in the universe. Because they are God-related, they live for a higher will than their own. Consequently they are able to use their own suffering as an opportunity to help others turn tragedies into triumph. Pain has become a tool for them. They are whole people.

What does it look like to have found your soul? Let me tell you the story of someone who made the pilgrimage successfully and found the promised land within.

At seventy-two years of age, Ruth Eaton became concerned for the condition of the forgotten "old people" in the nursing homes that surrounded our church. Certainly Ruth qualified for retirement. Her life had not been easy. Over the years she told me of many private heartaches during times of adversity, limited income, and personal stress.

When Ruth's daughter, Lula Belle, suffered an untimely death at age forty, Ruth felt crushed. Nevertheless, she never let herself become numb to the needs of others.

One morning Ruth showed up in my office with the idea of how "we" could adopt the discarded humanity that was piling up in these last human dump bins of our society. Singlehandedly, she set in motion an outreach that was to touch thousands of completely forgotten people with new joy and hope.

As the years went by, Ruth never flagged in her zeal to help the "old folks." She spent countless hours finding more people to help and scavenging funds to provide gifts and remembrances. Ruth spent thousands and thousands of hours writing cards, wrapping gifts, visiting homes, and finding entertainment for people who were not remembered by another soul in the universe.

I wish you could have experienced Ruth at eighty-four as she scurried about trying to get Christmas ready for about five hundred of the neglected. Her living room was stacked high with boxes. Tissue paper was strewn everywhere among piles of clothing, sundries, and houseshoes.

"Did you come to wrap or jawbone?" she greeted me at the door impatiently. "Time's a'wastin', you know."

"I thought you might like to take a break and talk about the distribution the youth will be doing this year."

"Coffee breaks are for you young'uns that don't have the stamina we did at your age. Come on in." Ruth reached up and affectionately pulled on my beard. "You look awful in that scraggly thing. I'll be glad when you cut it off."

"Some of us were a little concerned that you might be overextending yourself," I began timidly, "and I thought . . ."

"Ridiculous," she dismissed me with a wave of the hand. "Age is all in the mind and is too highly rated anyway."

With that, she handed me a box and went into another room to find some ribbon. Our concern for her health was dismissed as self-centered nonsense. Ruth went on like that up until a month before her death, which she saw as a necessary interruption in the flow of her life.

For her, death was a momentary inconvenience on the way to other causes. Her body wasn't in great shape that day, but Ruth's devotion to the needs of others had resulted in an inner world of considerable proportions. Ignoring her own irritants, she found her soul by filling the loneliness and emptiness of others.

Such is a portrait of true life. It demonstrates recovery and discovery. If I don't find my soul, I will become a forty-, fifty-, or sixty-year-old skin draped over a four-year-old's skeleton. Once recovered, the soul provides the pivotal point around which my life can turn, regardless of obstacles placed in my path. Meaning, purpose, perspective, significance, and wholeness follow. The soul provides the overall context which makes sense out of my life.

CONCLUSIONS

We have discovered the Bible uses three key words to guide us in our quest for serenity in a shattered world:

Heart. Spirit. Soul. These ideas are lamps for our dark nights.

Each concept helps me face life. The heart can surround pain with a new set of feelings. The heart purifies the past just as water filtration systems make rivers fit for consumption. The Holy Spirit empowers my spirit with new energy and creativity for the task of finding a redemptive way to use yesterday's errors and mistakes. The soul uses each of our problems as an opportunity for contact with the Divine so that even the worst tragedies can become the means to crack the shell that often covers the center of our lives.

Life helps me find each concept. Pain has a place. As heat warns of the destructive power of a flame, difficulty helps us avoid labeling the artificial real, the phony genuine, and death life. While it may be difficult for us to understand during the ordeal, our walk through adversity is essential to our maturity.

Pain has a purpose. Suffering can restore what can't be found any other way. We must be unafraid to face not only our own, but the difficulties and needs of others, if we are to grow, expand, and become whole.

- Catastrophes without a center or circumference can crush us.
- Once encased with meaning and anchored to purpose, tragedies are transcended.
- Without our unique wounds, we wouldn't have our unique gifts.
- Broken spirits are promised a new Spirit.
- Even more than discovering myself, confronting the soul is finding life itself.

Reb Saunders was right. "It is important to know pain."

THE
HOLE
LEADS TO
THE
HOLY

6

CAN I RECOVER
MY SOUL?

"Since I can trust you so completely . . ." (Ps. 56).

Whom can I completely trust? God? You? Myself? The thought of unveiling something as intimate, priceless, and critical as my soul anywhere at any time is staggering. Perhaps "all-that-I-am" will be mishandled and dropped like a clumsy tourist knocking a priceless vase from the shelf. Maybe you won't find me to be that valuable. Perhaps my grip is no longer steady. What will I have left if my essence is shattered? And if tragedy has broken me into a thousand pieces, I wonder if I have anything left.

No, I have to believe that the God who sent me on this inner journey will guide me along the way. He can be trusted to use every occasion as an opportunity for His best purposes. If I am to find true and full life, I have to venture, even if timidly, onward in faith—even when it might hurt. I have to believe that the broken pieces of my life can be reassembled.

We have found at least one truly valuable and persistent reason for adversity. God uses even what wasn't intended to change us. Suffering has an astonishing capacity to redeem us by the transformation of our deficits into assets; and the singularly most significant consequence of this metamorphosis is the recovery of our soul. However, it's much easier to state the principle than to believe the promise can happen to us. Believing that our pain can have value is difficult.

My tendency is to feel that the garbage that life has dumped on me will only ferment and become more rancid with time. Masses of people have gone to the grave

with their joy and dreams corrupted and infected by the
odor of what was never transformed. Our task is to make
sure we have found the process that can turn our rub-
bish into compost. We begin by trusting that, as God
makes autumn leaves into fertilizer for next spring's garden, He is similarly working right now to change what I
can see into something that I cannot yet perceive.

.With time we can make a surprising discovery. Treasures accumulate in rooms where all the trash had been
stored. In fact, many people ultimately discover that the
garbage has turned into gold. Could that happen to you?
I truly believe so.

I want to tell you something about my own discoveries and surprise in finding that some of the refuse
dumps of my past have turned out to be places where
the most important clues about my soul were found.
Like most people, I had lost touch with this vital part of
my being to such an extent that the subject was more of
a mystery than a memory. Yet difficulty became the
means of direction.

I am going to dare to trust you enough to tell you
about my soul and what I have found to date. The following is my testimony to the place of suffering in the
scheme of redemption.

THE JOURNEY INWARD

Remember the dream with which I began the first
chapter? Recall the haunting, constantly returning
scene of being left in a cotton field, which recurred night
after night for years? While that dream represents some
of my earliest memories, it took me decades to discover
how the whole episode was related to the displacement
of my soul. The dream's meaning was tied to the location
of my soul and was so hard to decipher because the symbols masked a grief that I didn't want to face.

Many adopted children struggle with haunting, unanswerable questions about their origins. Like many other
adoptees, I, too, grew up with the same lingering
doubts. When children are separated from their biological families, permanent fracture in their identity often

occurs. Even though I was quite young, a deep bonding had formed with my birth mother and my dream was trying to tell me that this issue was serious. Like a fault in the earth that is vulnerable to instability, my hidden, emotional fractures always threatened to create earthquake-proportion responses in my soul.

My garbage bins from the past were filled with fear. While generally hidden from my awareness, the fear of abandonment had crept into every dimension of my life. This dream was screaming at me to pay attention to the dread that I was concealing from myself.

The clinical name for my problem is "post-trauma stress disorder," which only means that I have a deep-seated anxiety about abandonment. Consequently any hint of being deserted again filled me with terror. Sometimes I dealt with the pain by being very defiant and occasionally destructive. At other times I went in the opposite direction and worked obsessively at trying to be perfect.

In the end the central focus of my life became the need to save myself by keeping life from going out of control. I developed an elaborate system of behaviors designed to protect me from what I suspected people might do to me if I let them get in a position where they could dump me. In such a posture I smiled, shuffled, and danced a lot, as if life were a bowl of cherries. But my inner conclusion was that the most I could expect would be the pits.

Periodically the earth within shifted, and the giant fissures in my emotions cracked open at two or three o'clock in the morning. Awakened for heaven knows what reason, I would realize that I was afraid of something that I couldn't quite touch or define. During the day I lived behind a protective shell much of the time. Unfortunately I wasn't aware that the real Robert and the front he presented weren't the same.

THE SABOTEUR AT THE CENTER

Why is it so difficult to see problems that are so obvious? An elaborate system of emotional protection had shielded me from my own fears. My anxiety had covered the axis of my being with an impenetrable shield. In fact, this formidable defense system had hidden my soul.

Carl Jung had a name for the mechanism that screens our fears from ourselves. He called this process the ego. Like having a little person sitting at the control center of our life, the ego keeps things under control. As I looked at my own inner world, I began to adjust my understanding of his idea. I found the ego might better be called the "disillusioned ego."

Let me clarify. Since ego is a word that has been used so diversely and loosely, it demands a clearer definition. Popularly, ego is used as an adjective rather than a noun. Often the word becomes a description of someone's self-centeredness or self-serving personality characteristics. Subsequently, self-assertiveness or overconfidence may be labeled egotistic. Please set these uses aside and think of the ego as a noun—a name for the system of behavior that we have developed to protect the soul from the abuses of daily life.

As the adrenal glands provide energy when we are threatened, so this mental procedure provides order. When reality comes pouring in upon us, our thoughts, feelings, and intentions are coordinated by this aspect of consciousness. Jung postulated that the major task of the ego is pushing out of view those experiences that are too painful, frightening, or threatening for us to face.

The ego, of course, is valuable. Without such inner strength, we would be overwhelmed by aspects of life that are beyond our management. In fact, when our memories or experiences are too overpowering for the ego to control, the result is described as mental illness. Paradoxically, the ego's strength is also our greatest weakness. Hidden experiences get lost but not resolved.

I came to think of the disillusioned ego as a little man who lives within, and from this point on I will refer to this helper as Mr. Ego. I see him sitting behind a large computer that resides at the center of my nervous system, scurrying around cataloging the events that are happening to me. He is coordinating their effects with the proper responses.

Mr. Ego is trying to make sure that I come off as a fairly socially appropriate person. When he does his job well, I look suave and competent. When circumstances overwhelm Mr. Ego, he becomes a frazzled, disoriented administrator who leaves me appearing nervous, edgy, and defensive.

Mr. Ego has a fundamental problem of not being able to trust anything. Nothing affects Mr. Ego's performance like fear, rejection, and shame. When these emotions pour in, he pushes the panic button that flushes everything downstairs into a secret file room where everything is stored under the label "Unconscious—Experiences That Didn't Happen." But nothing is lost. This material in our computer can be accessed only as Mr. Ego decides it is safe to do so. The clinical name for this process is denial. It takes years for us to discover that Mr. Ego has been playing a game with us all of our lives.

THE COP-OUT COP

Because of overwhelming things that happen to us in the early years of our lives, Mr. Ego is constantly frightened for our existence. The insurmountable delusionary problems cause him to distrust life, and he becomes a magician who is constantly making experiences disappear. This disillusioned illusionist is so skillful that in the process of doing his tricks, he loses sight of the real goal of his performance and makes too much vanish. Rather than helping us cope with, he causes us to cop out. When we can't face our experiences and their meaning, we are unable to face ourselves. In banishing the disturbing aspects of our life, he causes us to lose touch with our souls.

My dreams were the tip-off to what had happened because they were the material from that forbidden file room that had sneaked past Mr. Ego's surveillance. The sleep symbols appear in coded form in which forbidding experiences have been stored. When we decipher the images, we get at situations we have been hiding from ourselves.

The well-being that should have resided within our soul has been overshadowed by menacing specters of the past. Behind our inordinate drives are fear, hurt, and an inexpressible need for self-esteem.

Unfortunately, but generally, only as our lives are smashed do we get insight and find new freedom. Recognizing this fact helped me see how God uses our pain for redemption and transformation.

MR. EGO FULLY UNMASKED

Slowly but clearly I began to discover that the disillusioned ego is not so much an individual as he is a caricature of a real person. He is more like a system. As Ebenezer Scrooge became only a money-collecting machine or Adolph Hitler turned into a diabolical agent of destruction, I, too, had to face my loss of humanness. Through decades my ego had become only a reactionary defense system which I thought was the true me. Multitudes of people tragically believe their patterns of denial, manipulation, and aggression are really them.

In one of the classic episodes of the *Star Trek* series, Commander Kirk and his crew encounter a foreign spaceship that is threatening the galaxy. The aliens operating the ship seem to be hostile. When Kirk and company are finally able to enter the ship and break inside the control room, they find only a computer. The machine's responses are so human that it acts and fights like a living person. The computer has been programmed to function in a defensive, aggressive mode if an attack seems imminent. With no means of insight, the instrument will destroy everything rather than retreat. Although the system had taken on a personality, it was no more than a response mechanism. Therein is a parable.

Having lost our soul, we become like vehicles careening through the vacuum of empty space. Ever moving at increasing speeds, we are directed by this impersonal force that is programmed to react to fear, guilt, anger, or inadequacy. Our destinies cannot be recovered until we break into this computerized system and face its inhuman quality. To recover the real self, one must make a bold and terrifying decision to set aside attempts at self-preservation. We have to face how our power-oriented lifestyles are the product of our fear of powerlessness.

I began to see why many people are such poor examples of the faith they profess. For some, Christianity is just another suit of clothes that Mr. Ego wears. Certainly sincere in their convictions, the problem is that their values are artificial. The ego system still remains the dominant force in their lives. Periodically we read of some extraordinary person like St. Francis or Mother Teresa who has dismantled the ego process so that Jesus Christ is the true center. But tragically, the religious experiences of many of us are essentially only another change of costume. We put a spiritual cloak over the dirty shirt we need to take off. I am still frightened by how much of the time I am one of this crowd.

During the moments when I have been able to get behind the facade, I have been able to discover that many of my innate desires are very different from what I thought they were. However, the recovery of values, feelings, and ideas at my center is deeply satisfying as the quintessence of my being arises. The journey is difficult and often more than a little scary, but the recovery is more than satisfying. Only as we tread this path do we come close to the true meaning of being "born again."

THE ANSWER

While psychology is an indispensable tool in breaking down the door to the control room, I found that it is basically powerless to disarm the system. Having insight into something that we cannot control, we may only function with more desperation. While the answer is spiritual, it is not essentially religious. In fact, religiosity and religious activities often become just another aspect of the ego system.

Mr. Ego is quite willing to go to church if it shores up his procedures. As there are alcoholics, so there are religioholics. Religious compulsions can produce incredible activity and a fanaticism which only masks fear. People will attend endless Bible studies and listen to tapes, religious radio stations, and church music as a means to keep from confronting their fears. However, we must not substitute one compulsion for another. The answer is far deeper.

Mr. Ego must undergo a genuine transformation if his system is to be truly dismantled. Rebirth is the tearing away of the costume until in our nakedness we are ready to live beyond artificiality. In fact, the throes of anguish which visit us in the dark of night are often symptoms of a struggle for change that has already begun within us.

There can be no renewal except as the layers of resistance are peeled away. Of course, any form of stripping is exceedingly frightening and painful. But now we are in a place to see the significance of our suffering. Pain is the most effective stripper in all of human experience. For most of us there is little genuine change at the center of our behavior without anguish. Consequently the tragedies we must live through often turn out to be our salvation.

The difference between religious veneer and genuine spiritual solutions was profoundly expressed by Jesus. He said, "If any man would come after me, let him deny himself and take up his cross daily and follow me. For whoever would save his life will lose it; and whoever loses his life for my sake, he will save it. For what does it profit a man if he gains the whole world and loses or forfeits himself?"[1] We have to face facts. The goal of the ego is to gain the world for the sake of security. That pursuit must be given up.

Dying

Jesus taught that recovery of the soul is tantamount to losing the life of the ego system.

Far more than taking on some new form of religious behavior, the answer is found in relinquishing control of the center of our lives. More accurately, the issue is who will have authority over us. Paul expressed the change this way: "I have been crucified with Christ; it is no longer I who live, but Christ who lives in me; and the life I now live in the flesh I live by faith in the Son of God, who loved me and gave himself for me."[2]

Paul's description of "Christ-in-me" is more than a religious conviction that I develop. In addition to speaking of the work of the Holy Spirit, he is describing the principle of self-renunciation; I am yielding to a higher will than mine. The process is much like an alcoholic standing before peers at an Alcoholics Anonymous meeting and saying, "I have no control over my problem, and I turn management of my life over to my Higher Power. I die to everything that has been in order for the control to be transferred to the Father."

Instinctively we fear for our lives; Mr. Ego is truly a survivalist. Paradoxically, as we desperately try to save our lives, we lose life itself. However, when tragedy falls we are forced to realize that we never could keep nor ultimately control our existence.

The reason the Christian message has been such a powerful source of consolation to multitudes of people through the centuries is that as all of our support systems are destroyed, we come to the only source of life that endures everything. Jesus Christ alone is the custodian of life. The message of Easter is that not even death itself was able to keep Him down. Therefore, He is able to raise us up.

Displacement

I have preached the foregoing for many years. Standing by open graves, I have comforted mourners with these truths. While passionately believing the message, I had not realized the personal implications. Periodically I would see someone in crisis desperately throw themselves down before this promise. In turn, I was occasionally surprised by the immediate result in these lives that quickly exceeded my own experience. Confounded, I had never considered that in their total distress, they were in a better position to appropriate my message than I was. While I was living in the academic world of ideas, they were frantically floundering in the school of experience.

Now I saw the essence of what Peter preached at Pentecost, Paul taught at Athens, Luther debated at Worms, Wesley proclaimed in London, and Thomas Merton lived at Gethsemane Monastery. Jesus Christ must take the place of Mr. Ego and his system. This displacement is a conscious act of the will.

Direction

First I must recognize that I have lost touch with my soul. Second, I quit hiding from the truth about myself. When I have fully done these two steps right, I will probably be frightened to death to go on. At least I will be apprehensive about running my life on such a radically different basis. Third, I start to pray that the Holy Spirit will accomplish the change in me that I can't make by myself. I ask to be crucified with Christ in order that I will no longer live, but that He will live in me. I ask that a value system based on love replace the one that is constructed around self-centeredness.

Deliverance

And then I saw a new meaning to the Resurrection story. The suffering that jolts us into awareness does great violence to our spirits. My hidden, suppressed sadness had spilled over into my total life. The lance that had pierced the veil covering my soul had also cut me to the quick. I saw why so many people's souls died long before their hearts stopped beating. The tragedies that can bring us to rebirth also have the potential to destroy all hope, finally shriveling the psyche to a point that is almost beyond repair. Such displaced people trudge on as hollow shells that have become vessels of emptiness. Vitality has been stomped out. For a while I thought I would never again have joy in life.

But here's the good news. There is life before death. The Holy Spirit will restore our souls. Even as Lazarus came out of the tomb, so will we be revitalized. No one who comes starving and dying of thirst will be turned away unsatisfied. The more I dared to trust nothing but the reality of Christ and to depend on nothing but His provision, the greater was the spiritual reality in my life. When crucifixion is accepted and embraced, we are on our way to Easter morning. In a world which has the capacity to take everything from me, I have found what can never be removed.

CONCLUSIONS

I have found a new use for suffering. While I wouldn't have chosen this path, it turned out to be a way that was exceedingly valuable to travel. The conclusion I offer you? When everything is gone, you may be in the best place to find yourself. While we may not be able to solve the intellectual puzzle about the "whys" of our pain, we may end up being able to answer the riddle that is us.

Like a dynamite explosion in a pond, the violent concussions that send everything up from the bottom reveal what has long since disappeared. Only then do we have the opportunity to explore what has been denied. We can find the true us in the midst of the many disguises that we wear because in the tumult the ego is no longer able to control the soul. I can trust that God is going to keep me from being destroyed by the eruption.

So I have determined:

- As Mr. Ego loses control, I feel as if I am dying. Yet on the other side is true life.
- I have to stop hiding from life and retreating behind psychological and religious answers. Inner renewal comes only through authentic spiritual encounters with the Holy Spirit.
- We seldom know Jesus Christ as He truly is until we completely lose our support systems.
- No matter how bad the injury, the Holy Spirit will bring new life to our soul.

When we completely hit bottom, there is always something more down there to be found: the real you and me.

111

GOING TO THE CENTER

In the past chapters much of our journal writing has been concerned with what the Bible defines as heart and spirit. Now I want you to look as directly as possible into the nature of your soul.

So consider:

(1) Is it possible that you are mistaking activity for life, business for vitality, and sensation for soul? Analyze how you spend your time. Do you avoid the deeper and more painful issues of your life in the name of living? Do you use pace of activity as a way of avoiding facts of life? Write out slowly and carefully what you discover is true.

(2) Can you identify the signs of a civil war going on inside of you? At what points do you seem to be two people? Where might your soul be trying to emerge from beneath the layers of social debris and distraction?

(3) Is it possible that you have never looked for a "you" that is more than all of your roles, relationships, ambitions, fears, and wants? Push yourself to the edge of these aspects of your life and then see if you can find what is beyond. Seek to know how you are more than the sum total of these pieces that make up the mosaic of your lifestyle.

(4) Denial is difficult to confront. Inevitably we deny that we deny. It's important to revisit the sources of pain in your life. Go back and stop at these sites and let the difficult emotion return for a while. Make yourself remember what you would most like to forget. Can you get any sense of how you try to shut out painful thoughts and experiences? Can you begin to recognize how you have regularly censored some of the real you in trying to handle hard and unpleasant aspects of your life? As you are going through this exercise, make yourself look hard at the pain itself and at the patterns that you have used to escape from it. Write it all down carefully and thoroughly.

(5) You will be trying to explore what constitutes your Mr. Ego. What needs, wants, fears, and anxieties make up his system of responses? For example, I found

that the need to be perfect had been imprinted on me early in my life. So Mr. Ego expends a great deal of energy trying to keep me from ever looking like a failure. In most of us there is a desire to be unique and special that almost constitutes a drive. As long as we harbor such self-serving notions, we will find it nearly impossible to recover our soul. Write about what constitutes the game plan that Mr. Ego runs in your life. You need this in black and white because the ego system will do everything possible to deny the facts and suppress them as soon as possible.

(6) Ask the Holy Spirit to enter your life by offering all that you are to the purposes of God. Offer your pain and suffering for His use. Ask the Spirit of God to bring new life to your soul.

Don't fulfill this analysis quickly or in a hurried manner. Probably you will want to talk this over with a spiritual mentor or advisor who can help you carefully plan how the next step can have the most meaning for you. Usually a worship context is the most helpful place for this time of release. Make sure that you are truly emotionally ready and prepared. In some symbolic manner, literally offer your need up to the heavenly Father. Sometimes this can be done by burning a picture or burying an object in the ground. Often holy Communion is a powerful place for us to exchange our need for God's gift of new purpose for our lives.

PART THREE

Finding a
Light
Switch

SO WHAT WORKS WHEN I AM BEING WORKED ON?

7

AM I BEING TESTED, TEMPTED, OR TRIED?

"In God I trust without a fear.
What can flesh do to me?" (Ps. 56 RSV).

Pain has the promise of producing real personality. Rather than a pale reflection of the prevailing culture, our uniqueness can surface and unfold like a spring flower. Black and gray times will give way to color and a spectrum of new brilliance. While it may seem impossible during times of chaos and confusion, we can be changed regardless of how impossible it is to reshape past events.

If my soul is going to come forth, I must find some way to order the disorder as it is happening. While I am waiting for the image of Christ to take shape in me, I need to be able to sort out the ongoing onslaught of experiences.

"I don't understand," Tom began hesitantly. "I can't seem to find any place for the painful experiences that seem to fill my life. How can they be helpful in either developing my spiritual life or my soul?"

The hurt in his eyes was obvious. Tom was bright, articulate, and a deeply devoted Christian. He had diligently studied the faith and certainly put in plenty of time trying to share his convictions with others. But his life had been bruised and broken by forces that seemed to wait in the shadows biding time to strike again.

"I seem to gather disasters like some people collect stamps," he continued. "Sometimes I can see a reason, but generally I can't detect any pattern in what happens. Surely my experiences mean something, but I don't know how to react anymore."

Each blow that had struck him would be overwhelming to anyone, I thought to myself. I couldn't help but reflect on how many times life had dropped a bucket of bricks on his head.

Several years before, while preparing to leave the country for a new career abroad, Tom's father had committed suicide, leaving him the responsibility of caring for an invalid mother. Although the father had struggled with mental illness all his life, the weight of the terrible thing his father had done fell on Tom. Not only was he denied the opportunity to pursue his dreams, he had to wrestle with a sense of guilt about something for which he was not responsible. A string of bad experiences culminated in a girlfriend becoming deeply depressed and ending her life. Tom's experiences caused him to feel like a victim who in turn chose victims for his companions. "Yes," I finally said aloud, "it is difficult to sort out the meaning of these capricious, violent experiences that have been so purposeless and devastating."

Most of us don't have to deal with tragedies of such magnitude. However, we may have an equally difficult time in knowing how to respond to traumas of smaller portions. When an event becomes one in a series of catastrophes, we must have some emotional and spiritual source of insight or we may well find ourselves drowning in despair and disillusionment.

In the previous pages we have found that pain can become a way to recover personhood. No amount of tragedy can keep us from realizing that there is profound meaning to our lives. In one sense, we have come to see that in addition to serving God, there is something equally profound for us to do with our daily experiences. Every condition of life has the possibility of helping to transform us into the likeness of Christ. But Tom raised a new issue. How can I sort out and give some order to the completely chaotic explosions that happen along the way? To stay rational, I need some cubbyholes that I can at least temporarily use to store or give disposition to the intrusions that periodically happen to all of us. I've found three slots in which I place much that happens. They are labeled: Testing. Temptation. Trials.

ACTION AND REACTION

Frankly I have no clear nor easy answer to explain what happened to Tom. For the moment I want to leave the why of such tragedies behind. I'm not retreating from the issues, but recognizing a fact that's involved in the recovery of anyone who has been emotionally assaulted by such overwhelming experiences.

In everyone's life there is a point where all reasons, answers, and suggestions are completely exhausted. Circumstances are of a magnitude that is beyond rationality. To continue to pursue explanations would be like a surgeon who continues to probe a gunshot wound weeks after the bullet was removed. All poking will do is prevent healing. Even without insight, we often have to trust that healing is going on both physically and emotionally. Without such trust, our soul will stay hidden and obscure.

Tom and I knew we had arrived at such a place. For the time being, we must set aside the why and go on to how to cope. Later, explanations might have a place, but at that moment we needed to think about how he could respond to his problems.

It's important that you understand this decision we made lest you feel that the trauma in your own experience is being brushed aside—as if questions of justice, retribution, and compensation are being treated casually. No, there simply is a time to go on. We were trying to understand how to live with a wound so that the scar would have meaning.

Since I had no idea how these tragedies appeared from God's perspective, Tom and I began looking at his suffering from the human viewpoint. Often the attempt to build a mental ladder high enough to take a heavenly peek becomes nothing more than the occasion for a big fall. However, following the lead that the apostle Paul gave us in Romans, we could still believe that something was working in, around, and for him during these times. Discovering a way to respond could turn even ultimate tragedies into spiritual gain.

The more we talked, the more we perceived that constructive forces could work even through the worst moments. When the apostle wrote that all things work together, he was suggesting that we seek the possibility of purpose rather than brood over the appearance of chaos. We found that we could state that principle in an easily remembered form: fire and futility can purify and prepare the soul. We talked about how the purification and preparation process happens through three different ways of adversity: times of testing, times of trial, and times of temptation.

While sounding alike, these three concepts imply unique sets of circumstances. Each suggests different responses to adversity. Each implies a special set of reactions and interpretations. Regardless of what people have done to us, these concepts can help us sort out our confusion.

PURIFIED BY FIRE

Are you being tested?

While the designation certainly doesn't fit every situation, difficult times may mean that we are being tested. Testing is a critical process of examination which determines stability and strength. Value and durability are established. As with steel, fire is the means by which strength is added to metal. Since God has already determined our infinite value to Himself and clearly knows our limits, we might conclude that the time in the fire is to demonstrate to us what He already knows is true.

The Greek original for testing, *dokimon,* means "to prove genuine." The root meaning suggests that testing is an ongoing process in human existence. Fiery periods are normal in everyone's life. Testing is the rule and not the exception. No, we have not been singled out for exceptional abuse. Testing exposes what our soul is made of.

In one sense each day of our life is part of the rating process. Being made gradually stronger by these daily "weight-lifting" exercises prepares us for the more difficult periods by adding increased capacity to our strength. Extended periods of difficulty are essentially everyday living given to us in very concentrated doses. Here's the real problem. Will we have the insight to receive testing as a gift from God rather than as an unjust imposition of cruelty?

Like a good parent, God's love is tough, not sentimental. Committed to genuine growth and maturity, the heavenly Father allows us to have the full range of human experiences that are necessary for the development of authenticity. Every parent knows that the test can be as hard on him or her as it is on the child.

Following high school graduation, our second son, Tony, yearned to find his way into the world before he entered college. I recognized his need to establish himself as an independent person who was capable of making his own decisions apart from his parents. Highly creative, Tony had to find his own mind in much the same way that Indian youths found their bravery by going out into the wilderness armed only with a knife. To be an adult, a brave had to learn he could survive on his own. So we sent Tony forth for his time in the wilds. His decision was to take a six-month back-packing trip across Europe and into Greece. With sparse funds, he set out to see the world.

As we took him to the airport, I could see second thoughts mounting. At last we came to the final metal detector gateway and the moment of truth was at hand. The apprehensions in his mind were nothing compared to what his mother and I were thinking. Yet we feebly waved goodbye and with a forlorn look, Tony walked down that long hallway into the airplane and on to his destiny. Six months later a man came back down that same ramp.

The heavenly Father loves us too much to keep us from walking the long corridors of life. When the fires are kindled against us, we can know that we have reached the place where we are ready for the next step in the development of our soul.

Actually, testing gives meaning to life. We live each day in an arena where we demonstrate who we are. The test results are revealed in how we respond. The final judgment on our lives is essentially a gathering up of the data from all of these daily tests. Day by day, week by week, year by year, integrity and personhood are being measured. Purified or pulverized by life, we will generally be made stronger, more tenacious, and totally genuine.

Paul felt that God often gives us responsibility as a means to test our commitments (1 Thess. 2:4). We may be trusted with a divine responsibility in order that the very best will come forth in us. Through this testing, the authentic surfaces while the artificial and the unworthy are peeled away. While the process at times may be extraordinarily painful, Paul knew that what God produced would be worth more than any difficulty caused by the ordeal.

The remarkable story of Helen Rosevere comes to mind. She went to the Belgian Congo as a missionary doctor, working as a surgeon during the day. However, she was also concerned not to drift away from the life of the common people. Therefore, at night she worked in a brick factory alongside local residents. Even though her hands were tender and soft from scrubbing for surgery, she lifted, carried, and stacked bricks all night. Thus Helen Rosevere invested her years in Africa.

When colonialism ended and the Congo became Zaire, Dr. Rosevere was caught in the revolutionary transfer of control. Troops attacked her compound during the night. The next morning she was found beaten and raped. When she awoke in the hospital, she was in serious condition. Slowly the pain and humiliation came back to her mind. She found herself recalling all of the years when she had poured out her life for the very people who had now turned on her with the fury of hell. The "whys" screamed at her from every corner of her mind. Having given so tirelessly for the sake of Christ, why should she have been so battered?

As prayers of pleading poured out of her soul, the strangest response quietly and clearly came into her mind. The still, small voice said, "Can you thank Me for trusting you with this experience?"

At first the answer seemed to be a mockery. Then it became more like a mystery. As she slowly recovered, Helen pondered this strange oracle. What would it mean to thank God for a terrible experience that He had not necessarily visited upon her? Is it possible that one might be allowed to live through tragic circumstances in order that some greater purpose could be accomplished? Could it actually be an honor to be selected for such an assignment? Strange haunting questions indeed.

During the years that followed, Dr. Rosevere found the courage to speak honestly and candidly about her humiliation. Always fighting back the tears as she delivered sermons and talks, she allowed the world to look upon her violation. An amazing thing began to happen. Every time she told her story, women would appear. Their eyes instantly told the story of their own desecration. Falling in her arms, they sobbed out stories they had never dared tell anyone until this moment. In city after city, Helen Rosevere became an instrument of peace, reconciliation, and healing for women who had cowered behind memory's closed doors hiding their shame. Her experience became the means by which they became whole.

Of course, God didn't drop such a devastating experience on Helen nor are other similar ordeals His work. However, when Helen accepted the experience as a testing time, something was accomplished in her soul that changed her and the meaning of her suffering. A new depth of compassion, humility, and inner strength came forth from the crucible of her pain.

Having proven trustworthy, fire could only purify Helen.

But why must the testing be so difficult? From my own experiences, I have found two reasons. The issues are so critical that nothing must be withheld; our denial is so deep that nothing can be spared. On one hand, the product of testing is the perfecting of our faith and character. On the other, we are so subjective about ourselves that only the most forceful circumstances get our attention. The old story about hitting the mule between the eyes with a board before being able to give him instructions is painfully self-explanatory.

Subsequently there are a number of things that we can now see are accomplished by the purifying fires. Perhaps, most important of all, such times validate who we are. Our personal accreditation is certified. Far from being on the outside, these times of difficulty can prove that we are part of God's chosen people as was the case with Helen Rosevere. God is working with us because we belong to Him.

While we may not want to admit it and fight seeing the truth, we may deeply need the hard experiences that fall across our path. These tests may confront us with new promises that can be understood only in retrospect. Generally such tests come at the point of our strengths rather than our weaknesses. We are pushed to become even stronger.

Finally, testing can prove what is the will of God. It's not always clear what is artificial and what is genuine. Sometimes we cannot distinguish the permanent from the transitory. Testing plumbs the depths and reveals the core. The valid is sorted out from the invalid. When the smoke, steam, and clouds clear, we discover what will remain forever. Times of examination help us to see life from an eternal perspective. Such is the stuff of which wisdom is made.

So how do you act? What is at work when you are being worked on? Consider the possibility that you are being tested to become more than you have ever been before. Even our scars become assets through testing. Expect it. Welcome it. Use it.

PURIFIED BY FURY

Are you being tempted?

The Greek word, *pirasmos*, can and is often translated either tempted or tested. Only the context gives the clue as to which is the right interpretation. In the same way, only our life context can tell us whether we are being tempted or tested. Sometimes the test may come in the form of temptation; sometimes the temptation is a test. Either way, Scripture indicates that God uses both testing and temptation to accomplish His purposes for us.

The primary difference is that temptations involve *choices*. While tests occur, whether we acquiesce or not, temptations are clearly issues about which we must make decisions. Temptations are the result of our wants because some desire is aroused. The struggle begins when my passions are affected. When confronted with temptation, we must remember that our response shapes who we are and what we will become. If aspirations are strong enough, the temptations may come with incredible fury.

For example, Abraham was placed in the excruciating bind of having to consider killing his son Isaac as a living sacrifice (Gen. 22). The story begins by God either testing or tempting Abraham depending on how one chooses to translate the passage. Because Abraham was faced with a clear choice to respond to a command, I would translate this as a story of temptation. Child sacrifice was common in that day, and Abraham could have well reasoned that should this son be taken, God could easily provide another. This great chosen leader was hurled into a staggering conflict of great fury. Whom would he love the most? His son? His God? Because Abraham was confronted with a choice about his ultimate values, he was being tempted to decide who occupied the place of final loyalty in his life—God or the family.

There's nothing out-of-date about Abraham's story. While none of us would ever have to ponder the idea of human sacrifice, we are constantly tempted to put many things, situations, and people in the place that should be reserved only for God. Whatever is our final source of meaning and happiness is actually our god. Often people have lost their souls giving them away to something or someone who is less than our heavenly Father. In effect, we have placed God on the altar of success, achievement, accumulation, power, or even the family and have tried to slay Him. However, we, and not a ram, are the ones who end up caught in the thicket.

In the dark of the night when all the unseen forces of disaster are closing in with a fury upon me, I have to stand back and ask myself what I truly want and value in what is happening to me. Is it possible that I am being forced to recognize what I have previously not been lucid about? Is the real issue that I have been tempted and failed to decide correctly what is final and everlasting?

Matthew's Gospel tells the story of the temptation of Christ. While each enticement was a battle with Evil, the hand of God set the confrontation in motion. The story begins with the cryptic introduction, "Jesus was led up by the Spirit into the wilderness to be tempted . . ." (Matt. 4:1). The Spirit of God was the prompting force creating what was to follow. This setting is almost identical to the opening of the Book of Job. The first eleven verses tell us that the events which follow were set in motion by the Lord. The fury of Job's temptations had their origin in the will of God.

While we often describe the story of Job as one of supreme testing, there was a very important temptation that he had to face. The ancient story begins as we learn that Job is a righteous man. When his calamities fell, some friends came begging him to repent of his secret sin so that the heavy hand of God could be removed from him. These so-called comforters were spokesmen for what is generally referred to as the Deuteronomic Code of Retribution. Simply put, this was the idea that God always blesses the good and chastises the evil. Therefore, righteous people will always prosper and bad people will always get it in the end. The friends of Job were convinced that he was in trouble because of hidden sin.

As a matter of fact, Job was a righteous man in the eyes of God. His friends were wrong and Job stood his ground with them. He maintained that his punishment did not fit the crime. Yet here was a hidden personal issue Job had to face before the dark night would come to an end. Standing toe-to-toe with the Lord, Job proclaimed his righteousness and his right to vindication. Job was simply too good for such shabby treatment.

If we place Job in the terms of the last chapter, we can begin to see his problem in a different light. While he certainly wasn't a bad man, Job had become an ego-possessed person. He had lost his perspective. Who of us, even the very best, should stand before the holy and perfect God and tell Him what goodness looks like? Job had fallen to the temptation of believing his own press clippings. Mr. Ego had completely seduced him.

Sound familiar? It hits me between the eyes. How many times have I protested to God about how fortunate He is to have me on His team? Doesn't He understand that someone who has done as many good things for the cause as I have deserves first-class treatment? How can I be in this kind of difficulty being as wonderful and spiritual as I am? And when one is truly trying to be all of these things, the temptation comes with almost irresistible force. We become trapped by our own self-righteousness.

Job was finally forced to see that the answer was not to be found in his righteousness, but in a relationship with God. With all of his high character, he was to discover that nothing in his goodness exempted him from the trials of humanity nor gave him the right to question God. Only as he repented of his presumption was he able to find a new, life-transforming vision of the Divine. His only hope was in the constant care of the heavenly Father that comes to all of us only as grace. Job's temptation was to trust in himself. In the long night, he learned how to trust in God alone.

In each of these incidents the reaction of the one being tempted revealed who they were. Abraham was ultimately revealed to be a man of faith. When the writer of Hebrews comments on Abraham's predicament, he concludes that Abraham was willing to sacrifice his son because he believed God would have raised him from the dead if necessary (Heb. 11:17-19). The temptation only deepened the patriarch's faith in God.

As Job repented of his brash self-confidence, a new meaning of trust was opened to him. Now he could proclaim, "I had heard of Thee by the hearing of the ear, but now my eyes see Thee."

Jesus' confrontation with evil demonstrated how and why He was the Messiah. Not counting equality with God a thing to be grasped, He humbled Himself, assuming the role of a servant. Jesus completely side-stepped ego domination. He was obedient to God rather than serving the impulses for power that have always infected the human race.

In each instance, evil and temptation were made to serve God and perfect character. The fury only further purified each person.

At this point you may be saying, "Wait a minute!" Doesn't the Bible say that God tempts no one and He himself cannot be tempted with evil?" The first chapter of the Book of James does say, "Let no one say when he is tempted, 'I am tempted by God' . . . each person is tempted when he is lured and enticed by his own desire." So, how do we reconcile these two points of view?

We must recognize that James is a balancing book for people who have missed the paradoxical nature of the Christian faith and the human journey. James is warning about using temptation as a cop-out. In this sense, he is saying, "Don't blame your junk on God." When you don't control yourself, don't put the responsibility on God. The fact that you shot off your mouth, let your eyes wander, or missed the proper priorities mustn't be elevated to the level of God speaking to Abraham about Isaac or Job wrestling with his tribulation. Our inordinate cravings aren't from God. So avoid spiritualizing them. We must not confuse the urgings of the flesh with heaven-sent battles of the spirit.

Which point of view is correct? They are both right and we face both types of confrontation. While we face the fury of temptation, we must not blame God for our own inclinations. Any portion of the Bible must be seen in the context of the whole. But there's good news. The prospects for purification are tremendous. Paul understood how fury can also be a finishing school. He wrote, "No temptation has overtaken you that is not common to man. God is faithful, and he will not let you be tempted beyond your strength, but with the temptation will also provide the way of escape, that you may be able to endure it."[1]

As exemplified by Abraham, Job, and Jesus, the "escape" is the opportunity to demonstrate who God has called us to be. In recovering perspective, restraining egotism, and resisting compromise, the temptation actually opened the door for final fulfillment to be found. The temptation isn't meant to be a snare, but an education in escaping all pitfalls.

The issue? Our choices. Our reactions. What happens to us is not nearly as important as how we receive it and what we do with it.

PREPARED BY FIRE AND FURY

Are you being tried?

While living under the worst circumstances and facing death, the apostle Peter wrote, "Beloved, do not be surprised at the fiery ordeal which comes upon you to prove you, as though something strange were happening to you. But rejoice in so far as you share Christ's sufferings, that you may also rejoice and be glad when his glory is revealed" (1 Pet. 4:12-13).

Peter was trying to escape Nero and we're trying to survive the IRS. He wanted to avoid the colosseum and we want to get off the freeways. He worried about Roman soldiers and we're concerned with the bomb. Perhaps little has changed through the centuries.

Trial by combat is still with us. While we no longer come at each other with swords and axes (generally), daily we have to walk through the fire. Often we talk about how we are facing a "time of trial."

These are periods when what we value is on trial, revealing what is true, enduring, and trustworthy. Our tenacity or frailty is exposed. Such crossroad moments arise when our previously divergent paths cross in decisive moments of disclosure. Suddenly the shakiness of everything that we thought was certain is revealed. Nothing is final or settled until we pass beyond this place. Once the verdict is rendered, we know the truth about ourselves as never before. These junctions are always an experience of pain.

I'd like you to consider two varieties of adversity. The first is the relatively normal everyday variety of being pushed to our limits. Wives, husbands, children, employers, friends, in-laws, and a cast of multitudes that we face every day at grocery stores and laundromats seem designed to keep us in a perpetual stress test. Most of the time we can look back and see these strains with some degree of humor as having been good for us. The hassles of life have a certain abrasive effect that buff the rough edges of our personalities and mellow us. The second type of confrontation, called the fiery ordeal, is what we must examine much more seriously. These are conflicts that help bring both recovery of the soul and restoration of our integrity.

Peter tells us there is a particularly important dimension to these times because these trials bring the potential to share in the suffering of Christ. Such tribulations transcend the small niche in which we live and lift us up to become part of the eternal task of the redemption of the world. The soul is quickened and expanded. These awesome periods allow us to be one with the Divine Redeemer in his mission. Surely such a possibility transforms the meaning of any affliction. When we find our problems can honestly be considered to have this character, we can, indeed, rejoice.

Holy trials generally come in a number of predictable ways. Often our commitment to principle—even if misunderstood—sets the stage for us to be tested. This happened to me after I returned from a trip to South Africa. Before leaving, I listened to many American businessmen with financial interests in South Africa who told me why Christians should keep out of politics and not call for sanctions to help the black population. Of course, the business people had never been there as they had only sent their money for them.

As vice president of the general synod of our church, I went to take a look and bring a report back to our constituency. As a matter of principle, I felt I should stay with the oppressed black people. Although it is forbidden, I spent my nights in places like Crossroads, Umlazia, and Soweto. I slept where the vast majority of the population of South Africa rests every night. What I personally experienced of cruelty, injustice, and inhumane treatment of human beings profoundly marked my life.

One morning around 4:30 I woke up in a little village just outside the city of Durbin. I seemed to be having a terrible dream in which I could hear multitudes of voices moaning and crying out. The sound was so awful that I sat up in bed trying to shake off the dream. Only then did I sense that I seemed to be hearing real sounds as if from some distant place. Trying to settle this strange experience, I had an eerie sensation that I was hearing the earth itself in agony.

I had decided I was probably overlooking some obvious explanation when I heard movement in the kitchen that invited me to get up. I found the family was around the table already dressed and very somber. While none had heard the strange sounds, they had received a terrible message. While we were sleeping, seven village teenagers had been forcefully taken from their homes. Each had been killed right up the street from this house and their bodies left in a ditch. For political reasons, these children had been assassinated. Later, as I stood by seven fresh graves, I knew that what I had heard was the earth weeping for the slain.

Obviously I could not return from such experiences and not speak of what I had seen. Somewhat to my surprise, I found that many people didn't want to hear these stories nor did they want to see the pictures I had taken of the conditions of squalor where I had lived. When my experience didn't coincide with their political pre-judgments, they became angry and told me I should never have stayed in those terrible places. Other people said I shouldn't talk about conditions they couldn't change as they didn't want to have to think about un-pleasant matters. Several people left saying that they didn't want to be in a church where religion and politics were mixed. Apparently deaths of children, splitting of families, poverty, injustice, and police violence weren't fit subjects for our quiet, upper middle class, religious gatherings.

This opposition to my sharing wasn't really onerous persecution; certainly not worth mentioning in compari-son with what I had left behind with my black brethren in Cape Town and the Home Lands. Perhaps I shouldn't even speak of it as a trial in the same breath as I speak of those living with state-inspired terror. However, as I re-member Bishop Tutu and other black leaders urging me to tell Americans that they would gladly bear the pain of sanctions in order to bring change, I can tell you that these courageous leaders, like my colleague Allen Bosak, are in a time of holy trial. Their commitment to following Jesus Christ to the cross that awaits them in public jails is a contemporary story of human sacri-fice by political tyranny. Surely they face a fiery or-deal which will prepare their souls to take on a shape that is found only with the martyrs in eternity.

Being misunderstood and persecuted for the sake of truth is a lonely path. However, when we walk down that street, we know a camaraderie with Christ that is found on no other road. Being either maligned or misinter-preted for the sake of principle puts one in privileged company.

Scripture indicates that all who follow Jesus as Mes-siah will face some form of persecution during their life-time (2 Tim. 3:12). Compromisers avoid this fire by simply stepping around the heat, but the devout will walk through the flames. These ordeals validate the reality of our faith, reveal our integrity, and lift up the soul.

Talk of persecution conjures up images of facing lions in the colosseum of Rome and secret police chasing believers down dark alleys. Since few of us live under such political conditions, it's hard to take the idea of oppression seriously even though Paul said it's unavoidable. So let me put the issue in a more immediate and applicable form.

Trials occur in economically pressed times when everyone else is selling out to the lowest bidder. You find out what your price is. What do you do when your dreams are being shredded, no one seems to care, and you are forced to stand completely alone? What decisions do you make when social tides change and you find yourself standing countercurrent to popular opinions? Such an hour can be your day of oppression.

On the other hand, what happens to your faith when you are succeeding beyond your wildest dreams? Affluent times notoriously result in apathy and indifference. And people living in a materialistic society swamped with indulgence are often tried by futility. So when all around you people are bored by noble causes and a world of needy people, what about your discipline, consistency, and commitment? If it diminishes, you're not facing the trial well.

Tribulations in the midst of opulence are important because the full truth about our ego and integrity can be discovered. Our illusions and idealizations are no longer important. The evidence that goes to the jury is what counts. Often when facts are on the table, the evidence isn't very flattering or the answer satisfying. Even if we place a verdict of guilty on ourselves, the experience may have been a God-given opportunity for insight that will help us regroup. Once we see the truth, we are in a position to correct our course and start over again.

The trials the Holy Spirit leads us through are never ends in themselves. They are divine operations that cut out cancers that have grown out of our distorted dreams, inadequate beliefs, and misguided values. Rather than damnation, the trial is treatment. Fire and fury are preparations for better things.

REJOICE?

But be happy about it? Is Peter serious? "Rejoice in so far as you share Christ's sufferings"?

In rare moments of extreme privilege, we discover that some trials allow us to participate in the suffering of Christ. There will be occasions that not only bring us closer to the full meaning of the cross, but allow us to become one with the Crucified. At such times we are admitted into the inner circle of God's chosen who work to redeem the world through suffering. Yes, such pain sanctifies.

Make no mistake: I am not describing some romantic notion of how glorious pain can be. Pain hurts, no matter the magnitude or obscurity of its character. But trials of integrity, tenacity, and long suffering grant such meaning to our lives that the value grows through the years until we cannot even count ourselves worthy to have had the opportunity to endure the excruciating experience that befell us. When we persevere, even futility serves our development.

Those who endure discover a marvelous result in their lives. Paul portrayed the effect as a chain reaction: "Suffering produces endurance, and endurance produces character, and character produces hope, and hope does not disappoint us, because God's love has been poured into our hearts through the Holy Spirit which has been given to us."[2] No one can buy, learn, or develop such character and perspective. Only living through times of trial produces the soul. The good news is you don't have to worry about being able to change. The transformation is done for you if you simply stay faithful.

Paul is describing the recovery of our soul through the process of pain. When trials expose what is superficial, artificial, and duplicitous in our characters, we are able to get free of the facades we wear to avoid seeing the real us. The ego is exposed. Only a work of the Holy Spirit can give us the courage to face up to the charades we play. However, once we've seen ourselves in God's mirror, we are on our way to a freedom that we would have never believed possible. Such is the power, the promise, and the possibility that is latent in the ordeals called trials. We are constantly being prepared for a better way.

CONCLUSIONS

Have I found an answer for Tom? If the task was to discover an intellectual rationale for tragedy, the answer is no. On the other hand, if the quest was for insight and perspective on how to turn ruin into reward, maybe some progress has been made. Our most fundamental need is always to know how to react constructively to destruction. We have found three boxes in which we can place our adversities: Testing. Temptation. Trial.

We have identified what is always the central issue: What has happened is never as important as how I respond.

Regardless of injustice, cruelty, emptiness, and futility, every situation can be used as God's opportunity for perfecting our characters and completing our faith.

- Fire and futility purify and prepare.
- Tests can prove what is genuine and will develop tenacity. They validate us and make us strong.
- Temptations purify and clarify us. We learn to resist and to overcome by choosing correctly.
- Trials prepare us for a bigger future and produce character. They teach us how to persevere and develop vision.

The psalmist was right. Trusting God without fear results in our not having to be afraid of anyone or anything else either. The soul no longer needs to hide behind the ego, but can profit from every situation.

GOING IN TO COME OUT

Let's go back to the journal you have been keeping. In the reflections you have been writing, you have been discovering important material about your soul. Now we are ready to add one more section.

Entitle the page Assessing. Then go back and slowly read everything you have written before you begin.

Now you are ready to draw some conclusions. Here's your question. "What am I becoming?" As I look at the good and the bad, the strong and the weak, what sort of composite do I see shaping up? What does the image of God look like in me? How am I being conformed to the likeness of Jesus Christ? What is the nature of the promise that is unfolding in my life? As you write, I believe you are in for some exciting discoveries.

PAIN
IS
A
PRELUDE
TO
POSSIBILITY

8

IS MY SOUL WOUNDED?

" . . . you keep all my tears stored in your bottle"
(Ps. 56).

Getting in touch with our souls often leads to another discovery. The night still persists within us. Our throes and struggles have opened up our inner world by ripping the doors off the hinges. Tears and slashes have been cut into the soul and time has not healed these wounds. The residue of the past is still imbedded in us like shrapnel from a fire bomb. We need inner healing.

Soul injuries are like puncture wounds. On the surface they seem to heal quickly while in deeper layers infection continues unnoticed until far more serious complications result. Unless healing is complete, the result can be worse than the original injury. While scars may be a sign of character and integrity, lingering sores mean disease.

To this point we have been trying to gain perspective on how all things will yet work together, trying to find a new sense of plan and purpose to our experiences. However, Scripture promises us more than just new perspective. The recovery of our soul involves the purging of old contamination as well as restoration of our God-given possibilities. The Father intends his children to get well.

When we have a broken heart, emotions are on the surface and feelings are tender. Although the situation is unpleasant, in time we find that hurts slip away until we are back in balance. Rejected love can be replaced by another.

It is more difficult to recover from a broken spirit. Years may pass before we are able to find the drive, confidence, or enthusiasm that was smashed when our spirit was crushed.

But nothing is as hard to restore as the soul. Perhaps

one of the reasons that the soul seems to be so well pro-
tected and hard to find is that damage here is far more
devastating. Often only divine intervention makes any
degree of recovery possible.

Healing must occur on a number of levels for us to
have the full life that has been promised to us by our
Creator and Redeemer. We begin with the recovery of
our perspective. We must have healthy insight into our
circumstances. But the next step is to go deeper into the
realm of our emotional responses. Guilt, anger, despair,
hate, anxiety, and fear are powerful energies that can
turn against us with devastating results. Runaway emotions have to be contained and soothed for us to have a
sense of well-being. The previous chapters have offered
help in finding new emotional health.

The soundness of the soul is another matter. Too often
we assume that reason and a little applied psychology
will take care of all that ails us. This conclusion is simply
not true. Beyond psychiatry and psychotherapy, restoration of the soul needs a more profound and yet infinitely
simpler remedy. Only the process of prayer can finally
cure the deeper places.

Unfortunately many people within the Christian community talk about a promise they don't practice. For
centuries the church has been filled with voices claiming
to be "new creatures in Christ," but sometimes there is a
strange silence at the level of performance. In stark contrast, the New Testament is a continuous narrative
about people who were set free. In the last thirty years,
many people in the Christian community have been recovering insight into what is implied between the lines
in the Gospels. We have become increasingly aware of
methods used by Jesus and the apostles in actually healing the soul and body. More and more churches are becoming hospitals for broken people rather than museums
to commemorate ancient spiritual victories. I want to
share with you some of these insights that help heal
wounded souls.

BREAK THROUGH—NOT BREAK UP

At various points in previous chapters, I have alluded to aspects of my own journey through the night. While I would never put myself in a class with many of my parishioners, friends, and clients who have been truly swallowed by tragedy, I know what it is to receive soul wounds. But my quest for relief began before I had any real awareness of my need. During that time I became aware of how to pray for the deepest level of personal need. I found it was possible to pray and find release through new approaches to intercession.

Often called healing of the memories, the combination of praying by asking, listening, and using the imagination proved to be the most important spiritual path of my life. I had the opportunity to discuss and explore this approach with Agnes Sanford who pioneered this way of praying. The wife of an Episcopal priest and child of missionaries to China, Agnes spent her life helping others recover. She was a phenomenal woman of prayer. Her faithfulness to Christ and sensitivity to others helped thousands experience what occurred when people sat at the feet of Jesus. She helped me see that we are still able to absorb and synthesize what the apostle Paul meant by "being conformed to the image" of Christ. The imprint can be an actual fact now rather than a hope for eternity. Our past pain is one of the best possible places to seek and find the transformation.

I had done graduate work in psychology and had been a social worker before entering seminary, so I naturally saw psychotherapy as the only available tool to help with inner need. As is true of many counselors, my pursuit of those subjects was actually a quest for the solution of my own needs. I knew the issues of my childhood needed resolution, but the idea of spiritual healing of my memories was unfathomable. Any good child of the Enlightenment learns, as a college freshman, that everything can be cured with insight and education. Later, time and maturity teach us that tragedy and trial are seldom helped much by either means.

Agnes had found that praying about pain brought the power of the Holy Spirit to bear on parts of our soul of which we generally aren't even aware. She recognized that the way in which Jesus prayed was far more imaginative than just saying words or hurling pleas into the wind. The unique character of His relationship with the Father was vivid, alive, and seemed to be more like a dynamic conversation in which there was both give and take. Christ's praying included encounter, involvement, and emotional connection that recognized all aspects of the heart, mind, and soul. Agnes discovered that the use of the imagination as well as the will and rationality seemed to be part of what produced healing.

HEALING THE INNER CHILD

My first experience of inner restoration occurred during a conference in my own congregation. Rosalind Rinker was teaching us how Agnes's method of praying led to healing. I had assumed the meditation was for the parishioners whom I had assembled. During most of the presentation, I was mulling over in my mind a number of things that needed to be done later in the day. Then we were called to pray about the emotional needs that had been discussed, but we were asked to do so in a different way. Rather than telling God about the hurt, we were asked to "see it," to envision problems, to experience past difficulties. By using our imagination, we were asked to go back and walk around in yesterday once more. I ended my daydreaming and decided to get serious about what the group was doing. I closed my eyes and sighed a prayer of compliance and willingness.

We were asked to pray that the Holy Spirit would help us get in touch with a time of struggle. We were to relive what happened by seeing ourselves once more caught up in our hurt. Much to my surprise, I found that a little boy of about eight years of age popped into my inner view. The little me was a deeply burdened child carrying a huge bundle on his back. He was bent and trying to walk forward into a pitch black schoolyard that seemed to be filled with terrors. I was startled to realize the symbolical form that my past had taken.

I knew the dark schoolyard well. As a child I had to walk across the foreboding place on Saturday nights where I always knew that some attacker was awaiting me. All the terrors of darkness were lurking there. The school itself was not a particularly happy place for me either. Much like my first dream of being left in an abandoned field, I had come again to a place that embodied all of the terrors that haunted the midnight hours in my early life.

From the front of the room in which I was praying, the leader's voice instructed, "Jesus Christ was there with you and you didn't know it. Ask Him to make Himself known to you now." Immediately I once more breathed the prayer, letting my imagination help me see what I might have missed in the past. To my amazement I began to "see" that a light was forming in the center of the darkness. As it grew in intensity, the form of Jesus Christ became clear. He was walking straight toward me out of the darkness.

Once more the leader directed, "Now ask Jesus to help release you from yesterday's problems."

Of course, I was aware that I was basically creating this whole scene in my mind. In one sense I was directing it like a writer creates a novel. Still, the contents were the stuff of my past so what was happening was not a fabrication or illusion. I thought I was firmly in control of the whole scenario. But at that moment, I found the experience took on a life entirely of its own and I became more of a spectator than director. Swiftly Jesus walked out of the darkness and reached out to pick up the burden on the child's back. Suddenly the whole weight lifted and vanished. The effect was so dramatically physical that I literally rose up in the chair, breaking the meditation. Astounded, I looked around the room at the rest of the group who still had their heads bowed. Slowly I became aware of a new lightness of being. I found I was breathing easier and felt a new surge of joy.

Only later did I realize what a decisive impact these moments had made on my life. In addition, a new dimension was opened within. Something new and vital had been released. The meditation was the first step in the journey to my soul and its healing. I found that I could forgive people for things they had done that I had carried with me for years. Genuine healing had occurred within my psyche.

BEYOND TIME AND SPACE

The issues of the soul have a timeless quality. Because healing of the psyche prepares us for eternity, the past, present, and future have to be dealt with as an eternal now. If the Holy Spirit is going to bring restoration, we must bring everything into the present. Although without much insight, that's what I was doing as I prayed with my imagination.

Let me explain a little more about how this approach operates by telling you how Agnes Sanford discovered this way of praying. Although she came to question the designation of this form of prayer as the "healing of the memories," the concept was developed out of her experience and writing. She had been concerned for a Jewish immigrant from Czechoslovakia who was deeply troubled. For almost an entire week she had meditated and prayed about the burdens he carried and how she might be of help to him. During this time she began to feel that the Holy Spirit was saying that the problem lay with the little child that still lived within him. "How," she pleaded, "can I help that little child?"

"You can't," came the response, "but I can!"

The next Sunday as she went forward to receive absolution and Holy Communion, she attempted to reach out spiritually and bring her friend's "little child" with her to the altar rail. Having spent a whole week praying for the man, she was remarkably in tune with his inner world. The result of that morning's intercession was a powerful healing work in the man's soul.

Later she reasoned that such a thing was possible because Jesus Christ is the Lord of time. Every moment, past, present, or future is before him even as this instant is before us. Hebrews 13:8 says, "Jesus Christ is the same, yesterday, today, and forever." As Agnes observed that Jesus Christ still heals today, she recognized that He can just as easily go back and touch the little child of yesterday.

At approximately this same time a significant book was written by psychiatrist Hugh Missildine. In *Your Inner Child of the Past* (1983, Simon and Schuster), Dr. Missildine wrote that emotional needs can best be understood in terms of how old wounds still reside in us in the same way they affected us as a child. The inner orientation still frames our adult perspective. The little child's wounds must be healed for the adult to be well.

Consequently, Missildine developed a sound theoretic base for what Agnes had discovered in her own prayer experiments.

Today we might call this approach a holistic method of praying for emotional trauma. The whole person, both now and then, is confronted. Introducing the presence of Christ into the past rewrites the person's history by adding Jesus Christ as the forgotten component. In the hands of trained or gifted people, this approach offers help that often cannot be found elsewhere. The soul receives ministry and release. I began to see that this type of praying was applicable to any point of need. We can confront not only the little child but the troubled teenager.

The effect of this form of praying brings the reality of love into the spirit. The soul is touched and bathed by the presence of divine love so the moment becomes like a lotion, bathing old wounds in healing medicine. When the soul is surrounded with love, we experience great peace and well-being. When our awareness of His love is low or depleted, life seems empty and we will feel depressed. If the condition lasts long enough, we can become emotionally and physically ill. Times of inner healing fill us with God's presence, and love heals the soul.

FROM PAIN TO POSSIBILITY

I have seen many people healed of the effects of past tragedies with this form of prayer. Watching the healing of a soul remains one of the most fascinating and satisfying experiences of counseling practice. Here are some of these stories that are instructive for our own needs. Let's begin with Mary.

"I can't remember when I didn't live under a cloud of apprehension," Mary said slowly. "The dread goes back as far as I can remember."

A bright, attractive, young social worker, Mary came seeking help for her troubled personal life. Although highly successful at work, her personal life was a disaster.

"I destroy every relationship," she sobbed. "I either let things get out of hand or I start manipulating men until there is no hope of anything good happening between us. I destroy all possibilities of trust and caring."

"I sense that you fear openness," I responded. "You seem to rush toward a cheap intimacy that corrupts every chance that you might ever have to become genuinely close and deeply involved with the other person. A lot of fear seems to be at the bottom of your confusion."

Her eyes widened and she reached for my hand. "That's it!" she exclaimed. "I act as if I want to be close, but I'm actually afraid. Something within makes me afraid to really trust a man. I try to sabotage relationships before they have a chance to make me vulnerable."

The infections of the past lingered far down inside Mary like unseen poison, spilling doubts and anxieties into her personal relationships. Her apparently long-forgotten injuries had an incredible ability to forever contaminate the present moment. Mary's father had died when she was four years old. She had felt abandoned and saw all men as untrustworthy. Her continuing fear of being left was ruining her life.

I assured Mary that the Bible has powerful insights to help us find release from the past. We read, "Remember not the former things, nor consider the things of old.

Behold, I am doing a new thing; now it springs forth, do you not perceive it? I will make a way in the wilderness and rivers in the desert."[1] When I suggested this passage held a promise for her problems, Mary was intrigued. How could a spiritual answer help a psychological problem?

I explained that Isaiah was painting a word picture of what would happen through the ministry of Jesus of Nazareth. As the Messiah, Jesus had the ability to turn the wilderness places in people's lives into blooming gardens of joy. The dryness and barrenness of their pasts could be transformed by rivers of living water.

"How can that be?" she asked eagerly. "How can something that happened two thousand years ago still apply to me?"

"Through the Holy Spirit," I answered. "What Jesus did for people then continues today. Like the air we breathe, His Spirit has the capacity to reach deep down inside. The Bible tells us that because Jesus the Christ is eternal, we can have the same experience that people had in Galilee."

"Well," she said leaning forward, "how can that happen to me? I can recognize my problem, but I don't know how to change!"

I pointed out that the emphasis in the nineteenth verse was on perception. The healing work of the Holy Spirit is not a matter of what we know as much as what we are willing to trust. I carefully explained that the power of faith isn't released through our understanding as much as it is through placing our trust in the power of Christ. Mary only needed to open herself and her emotions for Him to do the work.

"It's like breathing!" Suddenly she grasped the idea. "You're saying I should just open my mind or feelings to allow Jesus' Spirit to come in and touch my memories."

"Exactly," I smiled. "If you will expose the desert places in your past, He will do the rest. You still have a little four-year-old child living inside you. She is wandering around in a wilderness of fear and can't get out. Every time you get close to someone, she retreats in fear. This disillusioned little girl is destroying your present chances for happiness. We need to have Jesus Christ touch this child of your past."

"How do we bring this little child before Jesus?" she implored. "How can I let the Holy Spirit work with me?"

"I want you to both pray and use your imagination. Let me guide you in both a prayer and a form of day-dreaming."

Mary settled back into the chair and relaxed. Suggesting she close her eyes, I prayed a prayer for guidance for both of us and then asked her to pray that the Holy Spirit would enter into her emotions and memories. I suggested she let her imagination take her back into her bedroom where she lived as a four-year-old child. We were going to return to the afternoon following her father's funeral. Slowly and carefully, I guided Mary's imagination around this room. We recalled the walls, the furniture, the mementos, and the toys, how she looked and was dressed on that fatal afternoon. After a carefully constructed time of reflection, Mary was back in her room immediately after her father's funeral.

"Remember how alone you are," I counseled. "Feel how bewildering the service was to you. Remember the dread and apprehension." Tears began to run down Mary's face. "Look," I said quietly, "at the door in your room. It's opening and someone is coming in. Jesus of Nazareth is coming to visit you! He looks just like you thought He would in His robe and sandals. Now He's coming across the room and opening His arms to you. In fact, He's going to take you in His arms and sit down beside you."

"Feel his warmth and love!" I said to Mary. Waiting a moment, I added, "He wants to tell you something. Why don't you just ask Him to help you with your fears? Ask Him to heal your hurts."

Settling back into my own chair, I continued to silently pray that the healing power of the Holy Spirit would do a wonderful work in Mary's life. For a long time I waited as she cried. Slowly but clearly there was a change in the sounds of her voice. A new sound of release and relief emerged.

Finally, I began talking softly. "Why not tell Jesus 'thank you' for coming. Thank Him for helping you. He is leaving now, but what He has done will stay with you. Let's thank Him as he goes back out that door." Quietly, I said, "Amen."

When I asked Mary if she could tell what had occurred, she was too overwhelmed to speak. Haltingly, she told me she would have to come back later. The moment was too personal to be shared immediately.

A week later a very changed young woman came into my office. Enthusiastically she poured out the story of an amazing dialogue that she had heard in those moments of her prayerful imagining.

"I was astonished," Mary beamed. "I actually felt Jesus' arms around me, and He spoke to me. He said that whenever I needed my father, He would be there. He assured me that my father was all right and I should not worry about him any more. Most important of all, Jesus told me that He would always be there. I would never have to fear being alone because He would be with me forever."

During the year that followed after that spring afternoon, Mary entered into a genuine relationship with a man. She also found her way back to the church.

Mary's experience of her childhood had been reconstructed. A new dimension had been added. Basically, it was a matter of daring to trust Jesus Christ with the fragile place of her youth. Any time we are in touch with hurts, we can practice seeing Him present to the moment. As Mary did, we can prayerfully ask Jesus to salve and touch those past times in our lives. It is a matter of asking Him to embrace the injury and anxiety. Of course, we should always end by thanking Him for having done something important for us.[2]

FROM POSSIBILITY TO PEACE

John had lived through a hell beyond what most of us could ever imagine. Born in the Dutch East Indies, he and his family were caught in the cross currents of World War II. At six years of age, John was placed in a Japanese prison camp where he was to exist for four and a half years. Today the Rev. John Moser is a clergyman in the Reformed Church in America and a good personal friend whom I admire greatly. His journey from prison camp to pastor is amazing, but his transformation from severe pain to profound peace is even more gripping.

Beneath the roasting tropical Indonesian sun, the little boy, John, was forced daily to watch his fellow prisoners beaten, tortured, and often cut limb from limb with Japanese ceremonial swords. Some people were tied over beds of fast-growing bamboo, which quickly grew right through their bodies. Of the six thousand people who entered the camp, only John and three hundred twenty-five survived. Sustained only by hate and fortitude, somehow John endured.

When the Kybers of the Royal British Army finally liberated the camp, the cruel commandant and guards who had run the camp were courtmartialed and sentenced to death. The task of execution was given to the survivors. Immediately prisoners descended on the officers tearing them apart with their bare hands. Little John attacked with the first wave of executioners. Feeling fully justified at the time, he was still never able to forget the look of horror in the faces of the soldiers as they were destroyed.

John could not shake his terrible memories. Worst of all, he was not able to resolve the guilt he felt over the death of the Japanese soldiers. His soul was buried beneath a pile of human cruelty and the debris of hate.

As the years went by, the emotional wreckage did not diminish. Unable to talk of his burden, John found no relief until he attended a conference on healing. He was assigned to a group of four and was asked to share a hurt in his life. He began reluctantly to talk about his past. Suddenly he found that he was able to tell the group his whole gruesome story. Moved by the severity of his situation, the other three participants placed their hands tenderly on John and began to pray.

As they interceded, John began a mental journey back to that final morning in the prison camp. Once more he saw nine Japanese officers in their boots, caps, and tunics standing before him. Their faces were twisted and contorted with fear of their imminent, violent deaths. John felt the press of the crowd, pushing him on to the kill. Simultaneously he heard the prayers of his friends standing around him.

At that exact moment, as once again John was reaching for one of the officers, the risen Christ appeared in front of him keeping him from the assault. John began to "see" every detail of Jesus' robe, His feet, and His nail-scarred hands. Although the massacring mob was surging forward, John looked up into the face of Jesus. He saw nothing but wonderful, warm, incredible love. All-encompassing love had stepped in to intervene in the place of all-consuming hate.

To John's amazement, Jesus reached out and picked him up. He felt the callouses and the scars of the Carpenter's hands as He held John tightly. John could see the ugliness of the little boy whose hair was gone, his thin arms and legs and the protruding belly of the undernourished. As the little child of yesterday was enveloped in overwhelming love, John the adult began to cry and sob uncontrollably. Washed away by his own tears, he finally realized that the comforting Christ was putting him on the ground once more. Jesus then laid His hand upon John's head and shoulder and blessed him with peace.

When John finally opened his eyes and looked at his friends, he was staggered to find that his shirt, pants, and even shoes were soaking wet. He later reflected that it was as if rivers of living water had made him clean. Where there had been guilt, fear, and hate, John now finds he has a gift of love. Tragedy has turned into triumph for both big and little John.

CONCLUSIONS

These situations tell us how we can find reparation for soul wounds. Moreover, they give us insight into why some people seem to find a more dramatic recovery than others. Answers must go deeper than simply providing rational insight. Beneath the conscious mind lies the vast realm of the unconscious where we store all of the rubble and trash of the past. We must penetrate this realm to get the shrapnel out of our souls. Wholeness isn't possible until we have cleaned out the basement and the attic.

Psychologists have found that in the unconscious we arrange experience around traumatic events. Whether we think of storage as being upstairs or downstairs, the centers of organization are called complexes. These collection repositories must be faced if we are going to heal the soul. What we have been observing in the foregoing stories are examples of therapy for these deepest inner sources of need. Each person's experience brought light into their darkness.

Let's observe some principles that have operated in these inner healings.

- Our pain is anchored to a past experience. To get free, we often need to return to that time to find release.
- Much like daydreaming, we have the capacity to get back in touch with the centers of anguish. Like producing a display on a computer, we can bring up the past and re-experience our previous emotional frame of reference.
- While our conscious mind responds to ideas, the unconscious reacts to symbols. When we are envisioning or imagining an encounter with Christ, we are communicating symbolically with the unconscious and with the soul.
- Healing meditations do not create their own form of reality, but recognize an important aspect of the past that we have missed. During the ordeal Jesus Christ was there with us, but we didn't know how to call on Him. We are now adding what we failed to include.
- Though we can certainly pray for ourselves, often we need someone to pray with us. A spiritual director may be necessary and helpful.

- Always say thank you. Live in awareness that healing is a work of grace.

GOING TO THE CENTER

Few of us can live very long without accumulating significant inner problems. We need to act on the hidden agendas from the past. So I want to give you an assignment.

Write down on a piece of paper what you fear, or describe a situation that is difficult to face. Jot down some notes about why you are angry, what has made you hate, what you fear, or why you still feel guilty. Write out the description of your feelings as fully as you can. Clarify the problem using as many adjectives as you can.

Tie all of these feelings to a specific situation if you can. Be as precise as possible. See if you can remember the exact time when these negative feelings started to develop. The degree of accuracy with which you can frame the beginning of the problem will increase the opportunity to find inner healing.

When you feel satisfied with the insights, sit back and ponder what you've written. Often the next step will be immediately clear. Regardless of the justification for your anger or hate, the commandment of Christ is very clear. We are to love even those who are our enemies.[3] While difficult to accept, this commandment is also a principle of wholeness.

Inner healing almost always begins with forgiveness. We must forgive those who have injured us or have become our enemies. In addition, we must be willing to be reconciled with them. While that may appear to be a big order, it is still the path to healing for anger and hate. We cannot find inner health until these steps are taken.

At this point we need the help of the Holy Spirit. Most of us must ask for spiritual help to do what is emotionally difficult. Pray for that strength and then resolve to do what must be done in restoring a broken relationship, but forgive all those against whom you feel animosity. As you forgive, ask that your life be cleansed of all the residue that animosity has left in you. Often it helps to

153

visualize this cleansing. Close your eyes and imagine Jesus pouring out his Spirit on you in such a way that all corruption is being swept out of you. Let yourself "see" the inner moment of release.

Some people—like John—find they have described problems that produced fear or guilt. The Bible tells us that "perfect love casts out fear;" it could have added that love banishes guilt as well. We need to hear Christ tell us that He loves and esteems us, and we need His voice to penetrate into the unconscious.

At the bottom of our lives there may be a great emptiness. We feel worthless and unworthy. We may be haunted by guilt over what we have done and have a hard time getting the past out of our minds. We desperately need to hear that we are forgiven.

If this description fits you, you may want to put yourself in the center of this meditation. If so, read it through once more so you'll understand the idea, then let yourself quietly and slowly enter the meditation.

Close your eyes and see yourself in a large courtyard. Visualize that you are surrounded by all of the people or situations that now accuse you or intimidate you. Fully allow yourself to see into all of the faces that symbolize what has made you afraid or feel guilty. When you are fully in touch with the pain, visualize Jesus Christ coming into that courtyard. Watch Him walk across the way and past those who despise you. Look up into His face and observe the love that is there. Next, let Him say once more His ancient words, "Let him who is without sin among you be the first to throw a stone at her."[4] Now watch as one by one He turns aside those who would put judgment on you.

Finally allow Jesus to place His hands on your head and ask Him to fill you with the fullness of His love. Ask the Holy Spirit to pour love into every part of your past and your present. Offer to Him the tragedy and pain you have experienced. Simply sit in the light of His love and let yourself be bathed in what He gives. Fully imagine this flow of grace for as much as it is meaningful. These moments can be the beginning of the healing of your soul.

Perhaps a question has come to you while reading this chapter. How do you know that the risen Christ was with you through all of those long nights that seemed so empty? How do you know He was aware when you cried so much? Well, the psalmist has already told us that all of our tears are stored in His bottle. How could He have collected them if He had not been there with us?

PART FOUR

The Inextinguishable Light

WHEN
EVERYTHING
WORKS
TOGETHER,
CAN PAIN
BECOME GAIN?

9

IS THE NIGHT ENDLESS?

*"Because you have already delivered me from the
finality of the effects of death (which is the worst
that could happen), everything else can be handled"
(Ps. 56).*

But will the soul endure?

Inevitably we all must face the time when endless
night approaches. When overwhelming darkness comes,
what shall we say? When death is sudden, unexpected,
tragic, untimely, and without reason, what can comfort?
When the shroud falls around our place, words are im-
measurably hard to find. No one can escape such an
hour.

Though deeply dedicated people, Paul and Cheri Bedford were not exempt to the dark night of pain. Paul had
one of the finest tenor voices I have ever heard. He was
our minister of music and was looking toward an extremely promising career. In addition, Paul and Cheri's
second child had just been born. Nevertheless, Paul was
deeply troubled by his weight problem. Because of a
traumatic childhood, too often he comforted himself by
overeating. Unable to get the excess weight under control and bothered by his size, Paul decided to have a dangerous stomach stapling operation.

On Saturday morning his wife called me in desperation. Three days after the operation he was not doing
well and was in intense pain; even worse, the doctor
could not be found. By the time I got to the hospital the
nurses were frantic. No one knew quite what to do until
an emergency room intern ordered Paul to be taken to
intensive care. When the doctor finally turned up, Paul
was wheeled into surgery. However, too much time had
elapsed to repair the torn staple that had leaked infected

fluids into his whole system. Three hours later, Paul was dead. Even though the surgical procedure and the doctor were no longer allowed at the hospital, nothing could bring back Paul.

When I conducted his funeral, I looked down at his broken young wife, his baby daughter and son, and the shocked congregation. At only twenty-nine, Paul had entered the endless night. We needed a strong and certain message to ease the grief.

I began by telling the congregation the story of some other friends, the Rowseys. Jim is one of the outstanding eye surgeons in the United States. Daphne did some modeling on the side, but spent most of her time as a full-time mother of their three daughters. The many demands for Jim to lecture nationally and internationally kept their life filled with excitement and adventure. This beautiful family seemed to be living an idyllic life—before the medical reports came in.

When Daphne came to my office, I couldn't believe what she was saying. Cancer had come without any warning. The prognosis was fast, final, and frightening. Together we said, "No! It can't be!"

And so we began to pray with a fervor and intensity beyond anything I had ever known. We were thrilled when the disease went into remission. Our prayers seemed to be winning the war.

Several months later Jim and Daphne left for an extended trip to South Africa where Jim would lecture on new surgical techniques. I had almost put her condition out of my mind. But when Daphne returned and went for a checkup, she heard the worst. While they were out of the country, the condition had suddenly erupted, spreading like a wild fire. In a few weeks she was in the hospital with no hope of coming home again.

Some mornings are never forgotten. Daphne's final day will be such for me. About daybreak her vital signs had begun to drop and the end came quickly. A friend called saying that Jim had asked that I go to be with the girls. I rushed to their home to try and say something that might make a difference—or help—or make the excruciating pain stop for those three little girls. Why had this happened to my friends? Overcome by anger and grief, I needed someone to say the right things to me too. But what could words do?

But words do make a difference. The right explanation, a penetrating idea, a new understanding, or a truth we can grasp can change everything. While inevitably we feel the weight of addressing unspeakable situations, there are responses to be shared and light to be shed on these dark times. We need to know what the biblical answer is for death.

Death will always be the final frontier. No one can avoid the last adventure of crossing the River Jordan, entering the hidden land, and pushing on into the ultimate unknown. If the words of the psalmist are correct and we have already been delivered from the finality of death, then that's a promise we surely must claim and make our own. If God is working His purpose to achieve something good even in death, then we must know what it is. Since death is surely the blackest and longest night we must face, these urgent questions are the most important issues we must face. How do we get home before dark?

THE PROMISE

There was a time when we sang hymns about heaven, and public discussion of sexual matters was not considered appropriate. Today death has become the obscenity and sex is considered heavenly. Our current preoccupation with sexual appeal and youth culture makes questions about dying socially unspeakable and unbearable. Perpetual dieting and the new fad in cosmetic surgery are the best hope that multitudes seem to have for any form of self-perpetuation. We pay embalmers handsomely to make sure that if we should have to look at death, we can be reassured that "it ain't really so." When the end does come, we seem to be quite surprised that anything so unnatural and intrusive in the scheme and cycle of nature has appeared in our immediate proximity. Because of this mentality, we are unable to respond creatively and hopefully in the face of death. Moreover, our secular preoccupation with only what we can see and hear gives us no deeper perspective on death than a hole in the ground. When a whole culture has lost its soul, it's very difficult to have any sense of "something" going on beyond the last breath.

In stark contrast to our age of modernity, first century believers had a different mindset. While death was seen as an enemy, they believed the sting had been removed. They believed God was in control and divine intervention in Jesus Christ had changed how death was to be faced. God's invincible love had come in a personified way that insured continuity.

Immediately after Paul assured the Christians at Rome that God was maintaining a purpose in everything for His people, he described just how enduring His plan was. He wrote:

> Who shall separate us from the love of Christ? Shall tribulation, or distress, or persecution, or famine, or nakedness, or peril, or sword? . . . No, in all these things we are more than conquerors through him who loved us. For I am sure that neither death, nor life, nor angels, nor principalities, nor things present, nor things to come, nor powers, nor height, nor depth, nor anything else in all creation, will be able to separate us from the love of God in Christ Jesus our Lord.[1]

In order to face our own tragedies, we must know what produces such overcoming confidence. If we can understand and believe as Paul did, we will have the same victory in our own struggles with doubt, fear, and disillusionment. Why did the apostle Paul believe that the love of Christ was so invincible?

THE ANSWER

Paul had seen a light that the night could not extinguish. The most important ingredient in his convictions was the resurrection of Jesus of Nazareth from the dead.

The fifteenth chapter of Paul's first letter to the Corinthians is probably one of the oldest sections of the New Testament. Paul was delivering the first message of the early church exactly as it had been spoken by the first eye witnesses. His statements are a recitation of facts gathered from a wide range of people who had experienced the risen Christ. Peter, the other apostles, over five hundred church members, James, and finally Paul himself were all eye witnesses. However, Paul's account is particularly significant because his encounter came after the Ascension, telling us that experiences of the risen Christ didn't stop at some point in the past.

When Paul wrote that political systems, social conditions, natural catastrophes, personal problems, and finally death couldn't void God's ongoing care, he tied his proposition to a single bedrock premise. Jesus had been raised from the dead. Paul's conviction was his first and foremost promise. What had happened in Jesus Christ on behalf of all humanity had changed the possibilities of human existence. What the psalmist hoped for had come to pass before our eyes. For the first time in human experience, death had been defeated. Although written two thousand years ago, the apostle Paul was assuring people like my friends Daphne, Paul, and their families, that all believers are covered by what had happened in Jesus of Nazareth's death and resurrection. The answer is not an idea or belief but the consequence of a historical event.

But there's more to the story. The apostle John gives us a second dimension to the Easter story. John wrote about the meaning of life that has come to us in Christ. He said this existence is a gift that begins before death. While Paul assures us about the hope in what's unseen, John concentrates on describing the life that begins for us now. More than Israel's Messiah, Jesus brought a whole new order of life, which is filled with unending vitality. John remembered that Jesus said, "I have come that you might have life and have it more abundantly."

John witnessed how that occurred on Easter. He described how the resurrected Christ appeared to the inner circle, breathed on them, and said, "Receive the Holy Spirit." That afternoon each person entered into eternal life. They had found a quality of existence that continued without end. More than the "lightness of being," these frightened people now knew the Being of Light.

Later John wrote a letter to spell out what this new entry in human history meant for everyone in every age. He felt it was of paramount importance for people of the future to live with certainty. He said:

> This is the testimony, that God gave us eternal life,
> and this life is in his Son. He who has the Son has
> life; he who has not the Son of God has not life. I
> write this to you who believe in the name of the Son
> of God, that you may know that you have eternal life.
> And this is the confidence which we have in him, that
> if we ask anything according to his will, he hears us.[2]

Because of this statement, the ultimate fact of human existence is not death but life. Previously caught in a downhill drag that would finally dump us in the ground, now the unavoidable bodily winding down will finally release us from all bondage and limitation. Although occasionally slowed down—and sometimes knocked down—nothing can stop us from getting up and going on.

These two apostles describe how we can have life both before and after death. Eternal life doesn't begin at a funeral home, at a grave side, or at some future end to all human history. The beginning point for all human continuity is found in the risen Christ. When God spoke in Him, light was shed on all of our darkness. In fact, John describes Jesus as being a living Word that came to show us the truth we could never find by our own explorations.

The New Testament expresses this two-sided promise of eternal life by speaking of the survival of the soul. What we are is what we will be; what we have received is what will be given to us. The "real us" we talked about in Chapters 5 and 6 will be transformed and continue on just as Jesus of Nazareth became the risen Christ. All who have received life in Christ will come forth even as He did from the tomb. His victory will also be ours.

I find that it helps to recognize that we are living in an interim time. While the current moment is extremely important, we must balance it against what is to be. With that perspective, we can begin to see the deaths of our loved ones and friends in a very different light. Without diminishing the pain of their loss, we can see that nothing thwarts the ultimate purpose of God that they and we will be conformed to the image of the risen Christ. This conviction can lift our eyes above the shadows that fall when night comes and help us look to another dawn that shall yet be.

In the very recent past, some cynics and skeptics have called this message "pie-in-the-sky-by-and-by" preaching. Such intellectual and theological pseudo-sophisticates accuse Paul and John of ignoring the world of the here and now for the then and there. Such philosophers often condescend to acknowledge that promises of eternal life have a place in the Christian faith for the immature while the more fully developed could live without the need of such eternal assurances. Such *avant-garde* theologians have yet to stand by the grave of a child or spouse. Time and experience have a way of telling us the rest of the human story.

Recently I sat by the bedside of my mother-in-law during the last hours of her life. For thirty-three years I had known her as mother-in-law, friend, and parishioner. We had laughed, cried, argued, and shared the joy of children being born as well as the thousand and one things that happen between all of the Christmases and birthdays in between. Maureen, of Creek Indian background, had the heart of a real warrior and didn't go out easily. As I held her hand during the final death throes, I was reminded once again of how basic were Paul's promises that neither life nor death can separate us from the love of God in Christ Jesus. Nor was her final morning the first time that I had paused to reflect on how important it was to know that no amount of tribulation, distress, or peril could stifle the Easter faith. Having held the funeral services for my mother, grandmother, father-in-law, as well as both of his parents, I knew the power of this faith to hold us together when everything is falling apart. I did have a word to speak to the congregation that made a difference. I told them that day that death had been defeated.

THE EVIDENCE

Peter, Paul, John, and company wrote about their experiences because they thought that it was rational to believe that others could also be overcomers. Is it equally reasonable for us to hold such a faith? Is there any evidence to be offered to honest inquirers who are probing at the edges of human existence?

I believe there is.

The fact that Scripture has stood the test of over two millennia is solid evidence that the record has been true for countless millions from thousands of different cultures. Shrines to the veracity of the resurrection story have been erected all over the world in cathedrals, worship places, churches, and centers of culture throughout these past decades. The record of those who have been more than conquerors is enormous and endless. Because the accounts of the first witnesses have stood the test of time, I can hold the funerals of my friends and my relatives knowing that what I am saying has stood the examination of the ages.

But is there any contemporary evidence that the "finality of the effects of death" has been overcome? Are the ancient witnesses collaborated by our contemporaries? Is there anything more we can offer to the children of Paul Bedford and Daphne Rowsey that will help them see that the separation they must endure is only temporary and that there shall be another day of reconciliation?

I believe there is.

While I am content to stand with the Scripture and

personally feel no need for other footing, I have encountered a number of situations that I believe are also valid evidence. Personally I shy away from the esoteric and exotic as a basis for faith. However, as supplemental evidence to support what has already been written biblically, I have found that the following accounts have been of great help to people who needed some extra handholds and pathways into and through the endless night. I do not offer them to you as a basis for faith, but as corroboration of the victory that has been promised to us—
now!

Dr. Norman Vincent Peale, a clergyman of my own denomination, was one of the first persons that I heard speak of the certainty of knowing that the finality of death of a loved one had been overturned. In his autobiography Norman describes a moving experience that occurred the night his mother died. Molded and shaped by her life and faith, her loss was a source of great grief. Having received the news, he immediately went to his office at the church. On his desk was a Bible that she had given him many years before. It was his Sunday custom to put his hand on the Bible and offer a prayer just before entering the sanctuary. Keenly feeling his loss, Norman placed his hand on that Bible as he peered out the window into the night. Suddenly he felt two hands lightly resting on his head. Inwardly he knew that his mother was with him at that moment. Somewhere within his spirit he realized that his mother was telling him that she was all right and still loved him. Because of this moment, Norman was left with the absolute conviction that those who have "died in the Lord" are able to continue to love us and in many instances stay near.[3]

Remember the story of Ruth Eaton? Ruth was the eighty-year-old lady who took care of the "old people." Her extraordinary experience of the victory happened one morning while she was in her living room wrapping gifts to be taken to a nursing home. She was emphatic that I should share her attestation whenever I had the occasion. So, here's the data she had to offer.

I confess to having an abiding affection for Ruth. Two

types of humanity can do no wrong in my eyes: fiesty children and grandmothers. In my childhood the center of warmth was an adoring grandmother who thought I was wonderful. Knowing every naughty thing I ever did, she still offered unconditional love and admiration. Everyone should have at least one of those in their growing up. Ruth became an extension of my grandmother. So we were very close, working and praying together across the years. She naturally turned to me when unusual things happened to her.

I was sitting in my office with the door locked that October morning. I had told my secretary that even if the pope called, he would have to wait until I got caught up. Thirty minutes later the sound of Ruth's voice broke through the walls. I could hear her telling Jeannie that she needed to talk to me *regardless* and was coming through.

Having been down that alley before, I knew that I might as well put down my pencil and pay attention to what was on her mind. Ruth was not to be denied when she was on the war path.

This time as she came huffing and puffing into my office, her demeanor was different. Rather than her usual crusading charge, Ruth was clearly shaken, as if something overwhelming had descended upon her. While I tried to get her to sit down, she insisted on pacing the floor. She was not frightened or alarmed as much as she seemed devoured by something that almost defied her ability to communicate. I had the strange sensation that this moment was not unlike the problem of the first people who tried to make some sense and order out of the Easter story during the weeks that immediately followed that morning.

"Now you know I am a reasonable person," Ruth pointed her finger at me, "and I'm not given to a lot of nonsense."

I nodded my head.

"And you know that I'm very practical."

"Of course," I agreed.

"Then you'll understand why I have such difficulty in

understanding what has just happened to me this morning. We must take holy Communion immediately because that is the only response that is appropriate! I want you to have a communion service for me right now!"

"Now wait," I gestured for her to sit down. "What in the world are you talking about? We're not doing anything until you tell me the whole story."

She looked out the window for several minutes. Her eyes became misty and she sighed deeply. Slowly Ruth began to describe what had just happened.

Although it was only October, her house was already filled with wrapped gifts, packages, rolls of paper, and a thousand and one little items she had purchased throughout the year to be given to the forgotten. She had been sitting on her couch working on her nursing home ministry, tying box after box. As her mind began to wander to other times and places, she thought of other family Christmases that had been filled with family and joy. And now Ruth was all that was left of her family.

Her mother's face came into focus. Although her mother had died a great many years before, Ruth felt a sudden closeness and affection for the woman who had always been so dear to her. And then her daughter, Lula Belle, came to mind. Her sudden death at forty had been one of the great tragedies of Ruth's life. Because I had held her funeral, I knew how deep the wound was in Ruth's soul. Again Ruth felt a warmth and love for her daughter that had been suppressed during the preceding years of adjustment. As her devotion to her child surfaced once more, she began to travel down an unusual corridor of thought.

Ruth wondered how her daughter and mother were. While she believed they had gone to heaven, where was this place? Where were they? What was it like? Did they know each other? Lost in her thoughts and reflections, she had a strange feeling that she was being observed. Slowly turning her head, she looked toward the end of the couch and found that her mother and daughter were standing there smiling at her.

She stared, awestruck. At first she realized that they both seemed to be about the same age—around twenty-five. In life they had been decades apart in age but they now looked like sisters. In fact, Ruth was so taken with their close resemblance that she spent her first moments in overwhelmed silence.

While nothing was said verbally, Ruth experienced rapport as all of her questions were answered mentally as soon as she thought them. Yes, existence was wonderful for them and they were constant companions. Surely they anticipated her joining them. No, there were no recriminations or worries about the world they had left behind. Indeed, they lived in a state of peace that was total and constant.

Ruth was moved to the very core of her being. As she sat staring, she was also caught up in a form of understanding and relationship that was completely satisfying. The three women simply looked at each other for an indeterminate amount of time that could only be called bliss.

Finally Ruth looked away, trying to compose her thoughts for a moment. Suddenly she reasoned that it couldn't be happening. When she looked back, they were gone. Staggered by the appearance and disappearance, Ruth was undone. She left immediately for my office.

As I have reflected on Ruth's story over the years, the ring of truth has only increased. She saw an astonishing display of what the Bible means by the survival of the soul. Her mother and daughter were a demonstration of what the apostle Paul told the Corinthians they could expect. Ruth's experience fit the pattern demonstrated in the resurrection of Jesus from the dead. Is this valid evidence?

I believe it is.

Do you remember the story of John Faulk in Chapter 2? John was my son Tate's best friend. The death of this fourteen-year-old left a hole in all of our lives. But let me tell you the rest of the story.

John died the afternoon before Tate returned from church camp. When we picked up Tate from the church parking lot, he was filled with the adventure of his exciting week, and he had a hundred stories to tell. Immediately he could tell by the looks on our faces that something was seriously wrong. Slowly, carefully, sensitively, we told Tate about John. His face turned white and he looked as if he might go into shock. Tate was overwhelmed with grief, unable to find any words. Yet he felt the need to go immediately to his friend's family and express his condolences. So we began the long-dreaded journey into the night. How could we possibly find any words? What could be of any value?

The Faulks were one of those exceptional families of graciousness and high values that you like to have your children be around. They were a close-knit clan who cared about each other. I felt uncomfortable bringing my son to talk about their loss, but I knew they would be comforted by Tate's natural sensitivity and compassion. So we entered their living room, trying to search for the right, comforting phrases to say.

Much to our surprise the family seemed calm and serene. Although mourning, they had a composure that seemed to offer us more comfort than we extended to them. They were Christian people who believed all of the biblical promises, but there seemed to be something more. Finally, I commented on how peaceful they appeared to be.

George smiled. "Many people would have a hard time understanding what happened to us last night, but I think you will accept our experience. I believe you'll understand. I want to tell you about an amazing visit. Yes, we are devastated by our loss, but John himself has comforted us."

For a moment I stared at George making sure I heard him right. Carol also smiled as if to reassure us that they were fully aware of the implications of what was being said. As I looked at their kind, compassionate eyes and heard the steadied reason in their voices, I knew they were quite clear about what was being suggested.

"Please go on," I urged.

Chaos and confusion had come in an avalanche after

the message reached them about John's death. People poured in to try and help. Just sorting out the details of his death was chaotic. Finally in the late hours of the evening everyone left and George and Carol went to bed, where they talked for a long time. Although neither saw any prospect of sleep, they finally shut off the lights. Exhausted they drifted toward that twilight which is hardly sleep, but offers some reprieve from the day. Only then did George realize someone was in the room with them.

Looking through the veneer of dreaminess, he slowly recognized that John was standing at the end of the bed. Immediately John began to assure his brokenhearted father. Although it was unusual, he said that he had been given the opportunity of coming back before he "went on over." John told his father that an older family acquaintance who had died the year before was there to meet him and help him cross. He was okay.

Later George called the family of the person John described. They were astonished at the accuracy of what John told his father about this young man. George could not possibly have known these details.

John informed his father that there was a purpose and plan behind his death, but that it was too complicated and involved to explain. Apparently John understood the rationale for his death and accepted it factually as a matter of course. His parents were to know that everything was all right and were to go on living with confidence in the purposes of God. With a blessing, John indicated that it was time to "go on over" and went back to complete his final journey through the night into the endless day.

Two days later, as our neighborhood families stood around the grave, John's casket was set in place. The group of neighborhood buddies, including my sons, were pallbearers. A host of friends and relatives watched in grief as George walked up to the casket to say the final words. Acknowledging their loss, George spoke of his faith in Christ and the resurrection. As I heard his unshakable confidence, I knew I was listening to a man who was possibly more in touch with reality than any of the rest of us. Consoled by God's Holy Spirit, the Faulks had also been comforted by their departed son.

Here again was the form, substance, and shape of eternity that the apostles believed began on Easter and that Ruth had seen in her living room. The "soul-real-self" had not only endured but continued in the same knowable configuration as the person had been known. The terms of identity were constant. In each instance death's finality had been denied.

As I heard both Ruth and George describe what they had seen, I knew they expected me to be skeptical about their encounters. But in both incidents I was remembering an amazingly similar account that had appeared in *Guideposts* magazine some years before. Because the editorial policy of this prominent devotional periodical shied away from the bizarre, the story was all the more credible. I thought about J. B. Phillips' amazing experience.

During the afternoon of November 22, 1963, Phillips was sitting by his fireplace pondering the future of a difficult project. Having completed his famous translation of the New Testament, the Anglican priest had developed significant health problems. Because of the vitality and contribution of his translation, he was being urged to start work on a translation of the Old Testament prophets. The Reverend Phillips wasn't sure whether he had the stamina. Peering into the crackling fire, he was trying to come to a decision. Abruptly his reverie was interrupted by the voice of an old friend. He turned to discover that C. S. Lewis had slipped into the chair across from him. He was quite surprised as he had not expected a visit. Immediately the Oxford don began to encourage the priest. Yes, it was important and he should not delay his work. Lewis indicated there was a great need for an update of the Old Testament Scriptures. Phillips considered carefully the advice and finally looked back into the fireplace. Having composed a response, he turned back to Lewis only to discover he was gone.

WHEN THE NIGHT IS TOO LONG

The whole business of unannounced comings and goings was disconcerting. So Phillips got up from his chair and went to the phone to call for some clarification on this strange conversation. He rang the residence of Lewis in Oxford only to get his housekeeper. She told the shocked Phillips that it was impossible to speak to Lewis as he had just died.

Are these accounts reasonable grounds for comfort?

I believe so.

THE POWER OF TRANSFORMATION

In the twinkling of an eye we shall be changed; so the Scripture says. What we shall yet be does not fully appear but the clues are numerous. Transformation is in the wind. Where formerly death was forbidding, now we are dealing with the stuff of wonder and awe. The facts present us with the evidence of truly being more than conquerors of our final enemy. When Paul reflected on the promise, he concluded that what we have to go through now is next to nothing compared with the joy that lies ahead. Such knowledge conveys a power that will see us through the worst of circumstances and in so doing will also remold and reshape our present existence.

Occasionally the shape of this transformation pokes through the cardboard nature of everyday reality and we catch a glimpse of how awesome the plan of God is. These moments are parables in flesh, which keep us aware that faith is more than a set of facts we affirm. Rather our faith is a description of ultimate reality painted in colors too transcendent for the mere eye to see. When the night is falling, these shades and hues of total reality aren't affected by the darkness.

Stacy was such a picture and parable. I was the pastor to her family when she was a little girl. She had a strikingly beautiful, picture-book face, yet the gentleness of her personality was a delight unto itself. The effects of cystic fibrosis weren't evident then, but we all feared for the future. Because her mother's care was so thorough, we felt Stacy might escape the prognosis. Her father, Benny, provided everything money could buy for his daughter. Although there were bad times, Stacy fared amazingly well.

We moved on to another parish and the years passed before I saw the family again. Benny and his wife, Ginny, had provided the best, been incredibly constant, and had beaten the odds. Stacy was a teenager and optimistic about her future when I next entered their lives. Her family joined our parish and we started once more where we had left off. However, the disease had taken its toll. The characteristic thinness, blue fingertips, and circles under her eyes were telltale signs. Pneumonia was a dreaded scourge and any illness had frightening implications. Nevertheless, Stacy was determined to go to college. She maintained a courageous faith and was dauntless.

But time was Stacy's enemy. In the economy of God, she was not to survive the disease. Cystic fibrosis was a horrible adversary that cast a long pall over our many talks. We talked about it, prayed about it often, and developed an almost painful closeness. Stacy desperately wanted to live a normal life, and she gave it all she had.

College finally proved to be too physically demanding, and Stacy had to come home. Although we prayed fervently, sometime during this period she came to the conclusion that she was not going to get well. It was now clear that some evening soon the illness would be insurmountable. The time was not long in coming.

The last hours were very, very difficult. Benny and Ginny watched the final moments of their child's life unravel as she battled the inevitable effects of her illness until finally the struggle was over. Abruptly at that moment both parents experienced an extraordinary serenity. Peace fell like a cover over all the agony they had faced during the preceding hours. A new inner force sustained them.

They returned to Stacy's room for a final visit. To their amazement, although her agony had been all-consuming, Stacy now had a countenance of complete composure and peacefulness. Surprisingly a smile was on her face.

Benny looked down and began to recount Stacy's last words. As the pain had increased, the only thing she could say again and again was, "Jesus, Jesus, Jesus. . . ." Stacy had slipped into unconsciousness reaching out for the promise. An unusual thought went across Benny's mind at that moment. He had always wondered what Jesus might have looked like. Now as he looked upon his daughter, he began to have the strange sensation that his question was being answered. He was seeing Jesus. In alternating fashion, he could both see his daughter and the face of Christ. Stacy's battle with pain and suffering had taken on an incarnational character. Even in her death, she was wearing the face of victory. The risen Christ had so lived with them in her struggles that in her death Stacy's pain had been redeemed by His presence. Nothing—absolutely nothing—had separated any of them from the love of God in Christ Jesus and the triumph that He had brought. Stacy had been transformed by her struggle. And her parents had seen the shape of her soul as it would be for eternity.

CONCLUSIONS

The Christian faith stands on a very reasonable and firm foundation. Experience collaborates conviction. No amount nor degree of darkness has been able to extinguish the light that has come into the world. People who trust in Jesus Christ are delivered humanity. We have been promised that the soul, the real us, is not obliterated by death. Far more! What Jesus is, we shall be. We are a people of hope. Far from mere wish projection, our convictions are grounded in history.

So, we can conclude:

- The promise of eternal life begins today, not tomorrow.
- What we have through Jesus Christ here and now will carry us victorious to the then and there.
- The resurrection of Jesus Christ from the dead

gives us the shape and form of what we shall be.
- Occasionally the veil is turned back and we see the evidence before the fact.

We are to be comforted and to comfort each other with this information. A Word has been spoken to us and, on that basis, we are able to find the words to speak to everyone else.

*ENDS
ARE THE
MEANS
OF
BEGINNING
AGAIN*

10

CAN I FACE THE EMPTINESS?

". . . everything else can be handled" (Ps. 56).

We still have to deal with void when someone leaves us. Can we handle what we have to face? Sooner or later the tides will roll in upon us. Will we be strong enough?

In the last chapter we looked at faithful answers for confronting death. Understanding the promises for the survival of the soul is a powerful tool for rebuilding a shattered life. However, intellectual answers have to be turned into emotional fortification. Everyone needs practical direction in translating the pledges of faith into the path to endurance. We must focus our arsenal of insight to equip us better emotionally to face the emptiness death leaves behind.

Many people are defeated because they cannot find meaningful reasons for what has befallen them. In my book, *When There Is No Miracle*, I explored the problem of seeking an answer to the "why" question. After reading a small library on the subject, I came to the conclusion that there is never a satisfying answer to why our personal tragedy has happened.

In Chapter 2 we determined that the "whys" have to be turned into "hows." The issue that can be faced constructively is, "How can I use what has happened to me?" So let's explore further how we can release our pain so that it can be used for the purposes of God. This approach is the only satisfaction I've found to the riddle of our own catastrophes.

However, we still have the quandary of what our emotions keep doing to us. Recognizing that my calamity can be used by God doesn't mean that I can face it. How can I live with the emotionally haunting consequences that keep rising from within my soul?

Most often death and suffering are like the explosion of a hand grenade dropped into the very center of our being. The shrapnel lodges in our soul, scarring us for life. We need help in knowing how to face the blemishment and disfigurement that results in our damaged soul. If these damages can be handled, we need to know how.

The following are the personal stories of friends who discovered how to live with experiences that could have killed their souls. Their issues were not with hope of reunion in eternity but living daily with the absence of someone who left an unfillable hole by untimely departure. Their capacity to endure and overcome is instructive.

BLUNDERS, BUNGLING, AND BROKENNESS

Nothing is more haunting than the awareness that a few simple precautions would have prevented a tragedy. The ghosts of every form of oversight arise to accuse us of incompetence and carelessness. Facts are cited and recited a million times with each remembrance of the multitude of things that might have been done differently. The recall is like a scraping, scratching needle which only cuts a deeper grove in a phonograph record that should be soothing us with a song of consolation. When the culprit is a doctor, hospital, or some professional who should have known better, the lure into all-consuming bitterness is almost inescapable.

Probably the most difficult death to face is the loss of a child. When a parent dies, something of our past is gone, but when a child dies, a piece of our future vanishes. A wound is left that never completely heals. Often parents who have lost children struggle for years with the loss that can never be recovered. How does one face this emptiness?

In an earlier chapter I told you about Adrian and Maggie Purvis and the loss of their baby. This was a particularly devastating blow because the death was the result of medical error. The morning Maggie left for her checkup, she had a terrible premonition. Because of her own complicated medical history, it was important to follow closely the baby's progress.

On this day everything went wrong. Delayed by some problem, the doctor hurriedly rushed into amniocentesis not using the ultrasound that should have provided a safety factor. Suddenly the needle hit the placenta and the baby went into distress. Within minutes the dreams of the Purvises turned into chaos. The nightmare that followed took their daughter's life.

The issue Adrian and Maggie had to face was not a question about God's benevolence but about the bungling of medical science. Inevitably their loss was compounded by anger. What comfort did they have during these days of disaster? Later when we talked about their experience, we could identify components that helped them release resentment and find the stamina to turn back the finality of death.

The first step came at the hospital. Labor was induced and a baby girl was born. If it had not been for the trauma of the earlier procedure, she would have been perfectly normal. She had to be placed in an incubator with tubes running out of her body in every direction. Only an artificial support apparatus sustained her life. When the end was in sight, the family called me to the hospital. They wanted me to baptize the baby.

In our tradition the baptism of babies has no connection with salvation. Rather, baptism is the means by which our children are numbered among the people of God. Almost always it takes place in the context of a worship service. Generally I would not do what the Purvises were asking, but obviously this situation was different. So they gave their child the name of Brownyen. I said the ritual and she was counted as one of the Christian family. Later Maggie told me why this moment was so helpful to her.

"I know the baptism didn't make any difference to

God," she said somberly, "but for us it was a symbolic act in which we were able to turn everything over to God."

"We were able to place Brownyen in God's hand once and for all," Adrian added. "Then we were prepared to accept what we knew was inevitable. People need handles in order to let their faith work for them. The ritual of baptism did that for us."

Being able to release a person or situation into the hands of God is crucial for our emotional well-being. Carrying insurmountable burdens will leave us bent and depleted. Often we need a symbolic means of letting go in order to be truly liberated. Until the matter is relinquished, the effect is endless torture. If we aren't able to gain this release at the time of the problem, we must do it as soon as possible.

Baptism isn't a gimmick nor is it appropriate to manipulate its meaning to serve a different purpose. However, symbolic rituals can provide emotional release. Anointing with oil at such times has long been a ritual of the church. And there are many contemporary forms of relinquishment. Sometimes people will literally write a letter to God and seal it as a way of fully letting go of their grip on an irreversible problem. Often they write the letter to the person in the conflict. Many people need some way to act out their faith so that inner emotional infections are drained and healing begins.

The Purvises' second step was taken at the church. Although their infant had been in the world for only a few days, Adrian and Maggie felt it was important to have a funeral service and I encouraged them to do so.

Through the years I have seen how important it is for families to find closure on this time in their lives by having some form of worship, recognizing the value of even the stillborn. On occasion I have obtained a small casket for families, to minimize their expense, and I did so for the Purvises. Having secured the medical releases, I brought the baby in the casket to the church. This moment was treated with the same respect that would have been given to an eighty-year-old saint of long-standing church membership. Adrian and Maggie found this service was a significant time for them.

"I didn't know so many people just swept these matters under the rug as if nothing had happened," Maggie said to me. "This child was a person who had a soul. She existed for us and it was important to treat her life with honor."

In a simple but meaningful service, we celebrated Brownyen's little life. Together we recited one of the affirmations from the Heidelberg Catechism: "What is your only comfort in life and in death?" The congregation responded, "That I belong body and soul to my faithful savior, Jesus Christ." And so we recognized together that their daughter Brownyen also belonged. We put this tragic situation into perspective. While none of it should have happened, we looked beyond the error. Finality only applied to this world. From now on we would look at the facts from an eternal perspective.

There was a third step that the Purvises took. The cost of prolonged intensive care was a financial catastrophe for them. In trying to save their child, the Purvises had gone bankrupt. But because their disaster had been touched by grace, they felt a desire for a new and full expression of faith. Faced with a very real financial crisis, they concluded this was the time to start tithing. Adrian and Maggie made a giant leap from despondency to confidence by showing their gratitude to God through a practical demonstration of obedience and devotion.

Shortly after they began practicing new stewardship, they learned of a special fund which provided financial coverage for catastrophic illness. The Purvises do not offer a fabulous story of suddenly discovering hidden treasure, yet slowly they began to recover. Adrian later told me, smiling, "You can't outgive God."

While they were told they would not be able to have any more children, Rebecca was born eleven months later on the eve of All Saints' Day, which seemed comfortingly appropriate. Adrian and Maggie have now concluded that death became the ultimate healing experience in their lives. This couple have been able to turn their loss into gain, the night into day.

FILLING THE VACUUM

"I can't tell you how much this church has meant to me," Sharon smiled as she sat in my office. "Maybe another church would or wouldn't have done the same thing for me, but what I heard here week after week made the difference in my survival. I lost a child and found my soul."

I listened intently because I knew how overwhelming Sharon's situation had been. The only thing holding the Hernandezes' marriage together had been two-year-old Eric. His death also proved to be the end of the family. However, the nature of his death is the unspeakable part of the story.

What began as a routine childhood nosebleed proved to be worthy of a trip to the doctor. Everything see ned uneventful until the pediatrician mentioned that the condition was acting somewhat like leukemia—Eric's blood certainly wasn't clotting normally. As a precautionary gesture, Eric was admitted to the hospital for observation. The oozing still continued. Since he was in a teaching hospital, many medical personnel came by in the afternoon and evening.

However, no one took personal responsibility for the child and his treatment nor did it occur to anyone to check how much blood he was losing. The next morning when the nurse checked for his vital signs, Eric was gone. He had bled to death because of medical neglect in a hospital.

"The final diagnosis," Sharon said longingly, "was I.T.P., which is a simple problem created by a viral infection. At most all he needed was a transfusion of blood platelets."

"How were you able to handle the devastation?" I asked. "Such sheer incompetency is an affront to everything we all believe is trustworthy!"

"Of course, I was shocked almost beyond belief, but

several things happened that made the difference. The first was finding this church. If I had any advice to give someone in a similar situation, it would be to immediately find a church where you fit."

Although the Hernandez family hadn't even attended our church before, our congregation gathered around them with immediate care and concern. The church provided a support group of kindness and emotional strength. The next step was to help Sharon find her way to George and Carol Faulk's Compassionate Friends group where she could talk with people who were living through similar tragedies. Even though her marriage was falling apart, Sharon was upheld by people who were committed to the healing of her brokenness.

When we are wounded, most of us respond like hurt animals. We look for a cave in which to hide, hoping that seclusion will at least protect us from further damage. Unfortunately isolation is the last thing we need. While solitude has a role to play, we need to receive the warmth of other people. Certainly church atmospheres vary widely, but when congregations know about loss, they will be there for us. We need to be vulnerable to the possibility. Finding a supportive, loving community is crucial in being able to handle loss.

The second thing that happened to Sharon was a supernatural act of empowerment. Sharon received far more from the church than friendship. Something very powerful happened to her spiritually. "I was filled with new strength as if something had been added to me internally," Sharon reflected. "Within twenty-four hours of Eric's death, I had a vitality that I never knew even existed!" The Holy Spirit's presence was putting Sharon in touch with her soul.

While most of the rest of her family were falling apart, Sharon surprisingly became the center of stability. Even more amazing was the conviction that began to arise out of her circumstances. While she didn't believe that God had visited this terrible problem on her, she began to feel strongly that there was a purpose that He could realize through what had occurred. Sharon felt as if she wanted to set the world on fire by sharing the wonderful inspiration she was experiencing. She thought of opening her home to foster children or starting to work with high school youth. While having to adjust to a new aloneness, Sharon started living with a sense of hallowed connectedness beyond anything she had ever known was possible. While there were down days, Sharon had found the source of strength to handle every other obstacle life would ever hand her. How was this possible? The church offered more than human concern.

The church exists as the point of contact between divinity and humanity. These unusual-looking buildings with spires pointing to the sky are places where there are windows that open up into eternity. Churches are connectors between us and God.

The heart of God is particularly touched by tragedy and cruelty. If Sharon had been tempted to ask, "Where was God when my son died?" the answer would have been, "The same place He was when His Son's life was taken by the indifferent and the unconcerned." The crucifixion of Jesus Christ is evidence that loss, pain, and grief are experienced by the heart of God. Therefore, when Jesus said, "And, I will pray the Father, and He will give you another Counselor, to be with you forever. . . . I will not leave you desolate; I will come to you."[1] His promise was given to everyone who needs the strength of God. The windows are opened for God to breathe on our brokenness. Sharon had claimed this promise.

Sharon found that we are not meant to face emptiness alone. Those who hunger for companionship are promised a Counselor who will walk with them. Earlier she had lost touch with the religious dimension in her life, but to her surprise Eric's tragedy became the opportunity to find the Holy Spirit and reclaim her soul. Need became the vehicle for spiritual endowment.

THE EMPTY CRIB

With three beautiful daughters, Jack and Nancy O'Donnell looked forward to a boy to complete their family. Nancy was thirty-seven and the doctor didn't advise pregnancy, so they continued using birth control. Still, they prayed for a baby boy, and a month later Nancy conceived. This unusual setting made the chain of events that followed all the more contradictory.

On Friday before their son's expected birth, his heartbeat was strong. The final checkup showed everything to be perfectly normal. Jack and Nancy entered the hospital the following week anticipating a healthy baby. On Monday afternoon I was at home working when my wife called, telling me to get to the hospital immediately. Nancy was about to deliver, but there were no signs of life. The doctors were sure the baby was dead.

I was sitting next to the door of the delivery room when the stillborn delivery came. I could hear the confirmation that it was a boy as well as Nancy's crying. During the weekend the umbilical cord had freakishly become knotted, shutting off the oxygen supply. The unthinkable that seemed to totally contradict God's will and sovereignty had happened.

Many, many people came to the service we held for little John Lee. The congregation surrounded their family with love. In the beginning Nancy was wonderfully, spiritually sustained, but in time she began her inevitable journey through the stages of grief, resulting in a deep and serious depression.

As a psychotherapist, Jack understood, but also found himself facing a creeping darkness. Jack now recalls poignantly how women came to see Nancy, but that no one came for him. During this period both Jack and Nancy physically showed the terrible effects of the dark, all-consuming nights that covered them. The loss of the little one had left a huge hole. Could anything ever fill their emptiness?

Jack's recovery began with a passage of Scripture. His struggle with depression had turned into a sense of meaninglessness. Life began to feel absurd. At this point, a friend shared a verse from the Bible. Second Corinthians 5:7 admonishes, "We walk by faith, not by sight." These words became a source of reassurance for Jack that what he needed to find his way out of the emo-

WHEN THE NIGHT IS TOO LONG

tional morass was the trust of a childlike faith. God was holding on to him, whether he thought he could keep his grip or not. The verse told Jack that in time he would mend.

The death of his child also opened up some painful emotions from Jack's past. Parts of him felt as if they were dead. Shortly thereafter Jack had an amazing dream about a dead baby coming back to life. He felt that the dream was saying that what had been pronounced dead in Jack really wasn't. As he pondered his dream, hope flooded his being. The dream was a message from his soul telling him that something which he thought was gone forever in himself was coming back to life. As was so often the case in Scripture, the Holy Spirit used the vehicle of the dream to convey a message in a way that couldn't be missed.

Another healing dream followed. Jack saw himself in a cavern seeking a billion-dollar gem while walking through junk. Just before he came to the end of the dream, a huge sign appeared saying "Have Faith." He had found the priceless treasure. His own unconscious mind was assuring him of healing.

Jack found two key ingredients in the recovery of joy and meaning. Objectively the Bible gave him reassurance to which he could cling. The simplicity of the promise was stabilizing. Subjectively Jack knew how to receive his soul's response.

Dreams are messages of the soul that God often uses in His communication with us. The Bible is filled with many examples in both the Old and New Testaments. Having knowledge to read them or knowing a counselor who can help decipher these messages has enormous potential to help us be in touch with gifts of grace. Our souls have a unique inner bent toward wholeness and health. As we are able to allow this inner work of health to come forth, recovery is facilitated. Dreams are one of the most important ways we get in harmony with the means of recovery that are trying to surface.

Nancy's world began to turn around through a different set of circumstances. She came to see me in my office when the depression was at its worst. I told her joy

CAN I FACE THE EMPTINESS?

would eventually return, though it seemed impossible now. Subsequently, Nancy began to recognize that even though she was caught in a deep mental morass, eventually she would be all right. I remember her telling me that afternoon how her arms literally ached to hold her missing child. She had become extraordinarily in tune with people who couldn't have children, feeling their deep sense of loss. When Nancy began to use this awareness as a source of ministry to others, she started finding her way back.

A verse from Paul's letter to the Corinthian church turned Nancy's thinking in a new direction. "Blessed be the God . . . who comforts us in all of our affliction, so that we may be able to comfort those who are in any affliction, with the comfort with which we ourselves are comforted by God."[2] Nancy began to ponder how her deep realization of the desire for a child might be used to help someone with a similar need. As this thought was rolling around in her mind, Nancy became conscious of Joanna Smith's longing for a child. While the Smiths had been able to adopt two girls, Joanna's heart also longed for a boy. At that moment, Nancy felt a call and mission to begin fervently praying for the Smiths to conceive a child. Nancy felt she was particularly equipped to intercede. So she began to center on someone else's need.

From the moment she began to pray, she inwardly knew that Joanna would have her baby. When she timidly approached Joanna with the possibility, Joanna's response was, "Nancy, I'm afraid to open myself up to the pain of disappointment again, so you will have to have faith for me." Saying nothing, Nancy prayed, having the faith for her unfulfilled friend. Three months later the medical impossibility happened. Nine months later, Joanna gave birth to Ryan.

During her depression as Nancy had tried to read the book of Job for help, she noticed something that few people have seen. When Job began to pray for his unhelpful, critical friends, he began to be healed. Nancy's prayers for Joanna were the point where the depression began to leave.

While Nancy was explaining her prayer for another

and recovery to me, I recalled the admonition of Christ that we are to pray for our enemies. I thought of how empty it feels when we know someone not only doesn't like us, but wishes ill upon us. Yet I knew from personal experience how amazing the results can be when we literally do what He tells us to do. Emptiness is filled. Now I could see in a new way how *praying for another's problems actually brings the most effective spiritual relief to our own depletion*. I have found that in times of depression praying for others is one of the most effective ways to help ourselves.

The key issue for Jack and Nancy was facing the pain in their lives. The intellectual issues of tragedy weren't ever the problem that living with hurting was. Ultimately, they found their greatest solace came from developing a theology of the cross. "For as we share abundantly in Christ's suffering, so through Christ we share abundantly in comfort too."[3] The Scripture confirms that Christ suffers with us. This unfathomable mystery of the crucifix means that our pain is also always a burden that is lodged in the heart of God. No matter how alone we may feel, the truth is that the love of God is most with us in the worst of times. The growing realization of this fact began to lift and bring release to what the O'Donnells had to carry.

"Our society is geared to act as if it's possible to have a painless existence," Jack contends, "but only through the cross of Christ do we learn reality. We want a pain-free world and it's not possible."

Jack came to see that the ultimate objective is not to live as if pain is an illusion, but to learn through Christ how to find the transformation that allows us to use pain for others as Jesus did on the cross. As well as a symbol of redemption, the crucifixion is a model for mastery of life.

"I think I now know something of how Mary felt that day as she witnessed the death of her innocent son," Nancy continued. "I've caught a glimpse of the emptiness in her arms as she held the lifeless form; yet from this experience a new fullness has come into my life."

While the crib remained empty, Jack and Nancy recovered full hearts and restored their souls.

WHEN THE HEART IS SHREDDED

I had not known Bill Pulley very long when he shared with me the heart-rending story of his wife's suicide. Struggling with an emotionally crippling chemical imbalance, Darlene also had a background that all of her life had made her a high risk for suicide. Once the children left home, Darlene's inner defenses against her own sense of impending doom fell away. She could not find the tools to get well.

Friends and family lived with the constant fear of what seemed to be inevitable. When it came, Bill had the added horror of finding Darlene's body. Once he was able to stop screaming, he called his minister and then the police. How did he survive that moment and what followed? "But for my faith," Bill said candidly, "I, too, would be dead."

As Bill explained how he was sustained, I knew he had valuable information to help anyone who had to live through such a time. When his pastor and friend, Howard Cupp, drove him away from the house, the first question Bill asked was, "Do you believe this is the will of God?"

Howard responded emphatically, "If you really want to make me angry, keeping talking like that! Right now, God is hurting as much as we are and is just as upset." With that issue settled in his mind, Bill could go ahead and rely on the Christian convictions he had developed all his life.

"I really believe that God wants nothing but the best for us," Bill continued. "If the bad comes, He will make it possible for us to see how much good there is if we will look." Bill's positive faith and trust in a God of love was the glue that stuck the broken pieces back together.

But many seemingly endless nights followed. For a period of time, Bill listened to the recording of the funeral services over and over again. While there had been great consolation in the pastor's words, he was actually perpetuating his grief. Finally he came to see a principle that he had to apply to himself: *Pain is inevitable; suffering is optional.*

"It's amazing," Bill said with a smile, "how long people will cling to suffering when they can do something about it. I spent most of the first year praying to die. The second year I was still preoccupied with wanting to die. But at some point you get tired of thinking like that! I finally decided I had to put the past away. I had so many resources in God, the Bible, the church, and friends that I knew it was time to use them. I made the decision not to suffer any more. That's a choice we can make," Bill said knowingly.

Bill was stating a major insight that all who recover from tragedy must discover sooner or later. Pain is a bridge that we have to cross in this world, but we have to decide whether we will park on the bridge or go across to the future.

Bill's advice for going on? He suggests that people immediately start being honest about suicide. The social stigma is so great that denial begins at once and the result is that a high percentage of the victims never seek counseling. In contrast, Darlene's funeral service was forthright about the nature of her death. People who had been unable to face such deaths in their own families later thanked Bill because the services had helped them to be honest in re-examining their past.

"Suicide is a form of mental illness," Bill told me. "People have lost the ability to be accountable. Most certainly God understands the insanity that has consumed them and doesn't damn them. I am comforted in the knowledge that Darlene is in a much better place."

Bill was right. Taking one's own life is a personal tragedy, not a social *faux pas*. Saying the dreaded words suicide and mental illness out loud is important. We have to get inner reservations and shocking, unspeakable images out in the open in order to be free of the consequences that secrecy and fear create in our minds.

Ninety-nine percent of the survivors need a period of personal counseling. Talking it out is the most productive way to get on over the bridge.

A second hurdle that most people face is their anger at God. Since it's difficult to know where else to aim our despair, Divinity ends up being the biggest target around. Because tragic death is often interpreted to us as God's will, He gets all the credit and blame. While in the beginning stages of grief such a suggestion may sound comforting, later reflection will bring us to the conclusion that the Creator must be a pretty dangerous Being to act so capriciously and ruthlessly with human life.

Because Bill had always been convinced that the very essence of God's nature is love, he was surprised at the anger he found in so many other relatives of suicide victims. Finally he developed an approach to help the disillusioned. Listening to the vehement outpouring of acrimony, he would comment, "The god you are describing is a real 'son-of-a———.' I wouldn't want to mess with him either!" After the listener gets over being shocked, Bill continued, "but of course you haven't described the God I know. He's the essence of love."

Tragedy often makes us angry with God. We need to be reassured that our hostile feelings are normal and natural. While we may be afraid to face them, our heavenly Father isn't. He's big enough to handle our momentary rejection and belligerent emotions.

Actually, these times may be opportunities to break through our childhood images of the Divine and discover a far more realistic and adult view of our Creator. We need to remove the masks that we have often imposed on the face of God. Sometimes they look like the authority figures of our childhood. We are probably projecting immature feelings onto those portraits we have created. Often the resolution of our anger is the means by which we find the true God.

Bill believes the ultimate answer for a crushed heart is always found in recovering the reality of God. "He's there waiting for us to release what is creating the distance between us and Him. Stay on the hunt for healing." Bill concludes. "That's what counts!"

DEALING WITH LIVING DEATH

If there is a worse tragedy than untimely death, it surely must be a continuing state of deterioration and demise in which grief becomes perpetual. Not being able to go backward or forward leaves one in a state of suspended animation with continual emotional dissipation. Illnesses like Alzheimer's disease cheat life of joy and purpose while freezing loved ones in time.

I had known Leon and Carol Noble for two decades before the dreaded disease fastened upon his mind. Civic and church leaders, they were always a striking pair with a happy and vibrant marriage. Former chairman of his church board, Leon had been a stimulating youth leader as well. Following complications during surgery, Leon began to lose the ability to remember and to verbally respond. Quickly the ravages of the terrible scourge took their toll, robbing him of competency.

What should have been the prime of their lives became sheer resignation. The man with whom Carol had shared deep spiritual rapport all of her adult life became a ward. The overwhelming emotional and physical burden exacted a great price from Carol's emotions and body.

After twelve years of struggling with Leon's care, Carol reached the inevitable time when nursing care was the only practical solution. Following an accident that broke her hip, she was forced to face her limitations. Yet, having to give up responsibility for Leon's care was equally painful. The loneliness she felt apart from him was overwhelming. Would they love him? Care for him like she knew they should? Obviously no one was qualified to meet Carol's standards for attentiveness. Letting go also seemed like endless death.

Without realizing what was happening, Carol began

to lose perspective and slip into despondency. Her soul ceased to be alive and life closed in around her. Carol was spiritually sliding in the direction that Leon had gone mentally. She stopped coming to church, seeing many of her old friends, and began closing the shutters at noontime. At that point a passage of Scripture began to do a concealed, consoling work in Carol's spirit.

Carol returned to church on a Sunday morning when I was talking about the recovery of the soul. As she immediately recognized her need, she found that Paul's direction to the Galatian church was the answer she was seeking. "I have been crucified with Christ; it is no longer I who live but Christ who lives in me; and the life I now live in the flesh I live by faith in the Son of God, who loved me and gave himself for me."[4]

A new thought rang through Carol's mind. While she felt as if she were shriveling away, actually her diminished ability to handle life was the opportunity for the power of God to be revealed in her in a new way. Although losing her ability to control and manage life, the Holy Spirit was increasingly present to cover what was beyond Carol's reach. Stripped of sufficiency, she had actually come to the place of true empowerment. ·

While Carol had been highly aware of the reality of Jesus Christ in her life for years, her concern for Leon had obscured the meaning of spiritual guidance. She particularly felt the need to be in charge and control of every aspect of life now. Such a Herculean task proved to be impossible and it was killing her soul. As Leon's availability faded, she had to recover a sense of Divine companionship.

"As I got in touch again with what it meant to be in Christ," Carol told me, "I also realized that as He walks with me, He is also constantly with Leon. The ultimate responsibility for Leon's life has always been with God. Facing that fact allowed me to begin to release the overwhelming burden I was carrying."

Watching the attendants put Leon in bed at night had been very difficult for Carol. Her loss, fears for Leon's well-being, and lack of control over life itself were all symbolized in that moment. Carol's problem of perspective had arisen out of the pain of these times.

"I had forgotten that the Holy Spirit was still with Leon just as He had been with him when he was in a complete state of mind," Carol said thoughtfully. "Now I can be in peace when I leave home each evening."

Carol had discovered a practical truth. The heavenly Father stands on the sidelines like a kind, gentlemanly father waiting for us to fully request His help. When we choose to do it all "our way," He allows us complete freedom. However, when we reach the point of exhaustion, our cry of need brings His immediate response. It is as if He is saying, "I can now do for you what I would always have liked to have done if you had asked." *Carol found that living with this awareness of Christ's immediate help was what it meant "to be in Christ and Christ in me."*

Carol knows that she is still very important to Leon and that she also has a ministry in his nursing home. Each night she prays over him as Leon is being put in bed. As she carefully lays out his clothes for the next day, she continues to pray for the Lord's presence to be with him and the home personnel the next day. Carol has made a monumental difficulty into something that can be handled, and her soul has grown in the process. Today she blesses many other people who live in Leon's nursing home.

"The all-sufficient 'I' has been replaced," Carol smiled knowingly, "and I have a new center. I can be a living expression of Jesus Christ. He is working with, through, and for both Leon and me. I can do all things through Christ who strengthens me."

CONCLUSIONS

The loss of a spouse, child, parent, companion, relative, or friend always brings us up against the final abyss. From that bottomless pit seems to arise a cacophony of frightening noises, a terrible chorus of confusion.

Words like *emptiness, hollowness, vacuum, abandoned, left, alone, despair, deserted, destitute, God-forsaken* sweep into our ears, filling our minds with confusion and doubt that challenges every conviction. Nevertheless, we can handle the displacement that we inevitably experience during such endless nights. In this chapter we have found six principles which can help us turn faith into practice.

- Release precedes relief.
  We must turn the consequences over to God in order to get rid of bitterness.
- Don't park in the pain.
  Suffering is always an option. We can choose to go on.
- Keep your eyes on the big picture; frame "now" with "then."
  The facts of death are always meant to be seen in eternal perspective.
- Support is critical for survival.
  No one is meant nor able to face tragedy alone. We all need a community of support even when we are afraid of the intimacy.
- Offering up is a way of getting out.
  Praying for others, as you hope they pray for you, is liberating.
- When and what you can't, He can and will.
  Being in Christ is a matter not only of who calls the shots, but who carries the baggage.

No night is too long or too dark for the One who has seen the Light that does not fail. We can begin again. Everything else can be handled.

WHEN
EVERYTHING
WORKS
TOGETHER
PAIN
BECOMES
GAIN

11

CAN I RECOVER MY JOY?

"Even when I don't see it, your light is certainly always there. . . ." (Ps. 56).

Why do people suffer? And why me?

I didn't promise a definitive answer and no comprehensive solution has surfaced. Yet along the way a number of important clues have been found. As our journey together comes to an end, we need to make sure we have read correctly the road signs we have found. I hope we have uncovered a specific direction which applies to our personal situation. Each of us must be able to look beyond our own ordeal and put the shattered pieces back into some logical and plausible order lest we fall victim to irrationality. In this final chapter we want to make sure we are following the path that leads to joy.

What answers are there for the hard times? Why is life like this? Of course, the easiest and quickest response is always that we live in a fallen, imperfect, and incomplete world. Certainly true, but I dislike ending with this explanation because it is so negative. I am left feeling that my personal situation is a little addendum to a cosmic mistake leaving me only to make the best of a bad situation. I find this explanation to be as incomplete as the world it tries to explain.

We must find more satisfying meaning or we may fall into a trap that will only multiply our ordeal. A lack of significance is likely to create a personal rebellion against the experience of suffering itself. Refusing to bear our time of testing—and cursing its existence—can send us into an emotional retreat that will only compound our confusion. Trying to escape bearing the burden of pain is the ultimate form of self-deception and denial. In contrast we have found that by confronting the unexplainable and undeserved, we grow, mature, and become whole. So we need insight into the problem of pain that will sustain and inspire us to keep on crossing flooding rivers and facing rampaging forest fires in a universe that is frequently not user-friendly.

THE SECRET AT THE CENTER

At many points we have touched the edges of that creative mystery that is part of the enigma of the universe. As is true in childbirth, pain is often a necessary prelude to possibility. Far from contradicting both the power and sovereignty of God, suffering is part of the pattern. While we cannot find a lofty enough position from which to survey the whole, we have seen enough of the puzzle to know that we do not live in a crazy, meaningless world. Our failures, as well as our successes, have their place. Even tragedy does not negate purpose. Suffering is one of the components in the human experience, and it is useful.

The victories of God are won not only by superiority of position, but by bearing redemptively the inconsistencies in creation until love has reshaped each one into a new design and purpose. The ultimate symbol of this fact is the Cross of Jesus the Christ.

My friend, Heindrikus Berkhof, calls this phenomenon the defenselessness of God. The great Dutch theologian contends that Scripture portrays a Creator who does not impose irresistible power to make the creation bend. Rather, His nature is better described by vulnerability than obliterating might. The hallmark of God's love is His susceptibility to pain. The heavenly Father suffers.

As Deitrich Bonhoeffer faced death in a Nazi prison, he began to see clearly how God allowed Himself to be pushed out of the world by evil men only to return on a Cross. This martyred German churchman looked through the bars of his cell and recognized that only the suffering God is of real help to us. Bonhoeffer perceived that the seeming weakness of God is the very means by which He wins and overcomes this world.

The defenselessness of God is the very superiority of God. His yielding is not retreat, but the hidden and active working of an irresistible love. Because we have been created in the image of God, we participate in this strategy of victory. Although we often fail to appreciate and perceive the fact, He expects our partnership with Him to reflect this approach to conflict. Our capacity is not the inducement to crush, coerce, and overwhelm, but to endure, sustain, bear, and care until the victory of love has been won.

Why do we suffer? Because we have been given the awesome privilege of being able to care, sympathize, share, feel, agonize, empathize, laugh, hope, and love. Accepting the capacity changes the burden of the process. We are meant to be like the One who made us.

Herein lies a principle of recovery. Regardless of what has happened or the degree of inequity heaped upon us, when we make a decision to respond in love, though vulnerable, we are on our way to joy. Moreover, in returning love for injury we are becoming like God.

BEYOND JUSTICE

Unfortunately, our personal preference is for justice and retribution. Personal damages are carefully entered in a mental ledger where we keep our accounts of injury. When we have been abused, insulted, or impaired, we enter a debit, which stays on the books until a counterbalancing credit is found. In a corner of our mind we have all tucked away a little inner accountant who keeps popping up to remind us the books haven't balanced yet. More than just making us uneasy, he insists that we contemplate a wide range of responses that will get things back into even kilter by making sure that our adversaries get their "come-uppance." Our dissatisfaction usually results in some precipitous action that only makes matters worse.

Settling accounts can't do any more than bring acquittal. All the justice in the world never brought the dead to life nor turned bitterness into joy. The price for getting our pound of flesh is giving up wholeness and freedom from the ravaging memories of the past.

Only love heals.

What does it look like to live beyond mere vindication? Again the Cross is our best guide. The apostle Peter painted this word picture for us:

> For to this you have been called, because Christ also suffered for you, leaving you an example, that you should follow in his steps. He committed no sin; no guile was found on his lips.

> When he was reviled, he did not revile in return; when he suffered, he did not threaten; but he trusted to him who judges justly. He himself bore our sins in his body on the tree, that we might die to sin and live to righteousness. By his wounds you have been healed.[1]

One of the most accurate literary applications of this principle is Victor Hugo's immortal novel, *Les Miserables*. Jean Valjean's story is a tale of grace in the midst of injustice and insensitivity. A basically good man was turned into an animal by the brutality of the French penal system. For his crime of stealing bread for a hungry child, Jean was sentenced to years of imprisonment. Escaping, he eluded the police and came to the house of a Roman Catholic bishop. Starving, dirty, and crazed, he was about to be turned away by the frightened housekeeper when the priest saw the disheveled Jean. To Jean's astonishment, the priest not only invited him in, but gave him supper and conversation as an equal. Once fed, the priest also offered the convict a warm bed for the night.

No longer able to comprehend human kindness, the escapee lay awake, contemplating how to make the most of the situation. As soon as all the candles were extinguished, he sneaked into the living room, stole the silverware, and fled into the night. Quickly he was apprehended by the police who recognized the bishop's signet mark on the silver. Jean was returned for identification before being hauled back to prison.

As the candles were lit, the horrified housekeeper had her worst fears about the beggar confirmed. However, as the bishop acknowledged the silver, he carefully sized up the situation. Walking to the mantle over the fireplace, he picked up the expensive silver candleholders.

"My friend," said the bishop, "before you go away, here are your candlesticks; take them."

Jean Valjean was trembling in every limb. He took the two candlesticks mechanically, and with a wild appearance.

"Now," said the bishop, "go in peace. By the way, my friend, when you come again, you need not come through the garden. You can always come in and go out by the front door. It is closed only with a latch, day or night."

Then turning to the gendarmes, he said, "Messieurs, you can retire." The gendarmes withdrew.

Jean Valjean felt like a man who is just about to faint. The bishop approached him, and said, in a low voice, "Forget not, never forget that you have promised me to use this silver to become an honest man."

Jean Valjean, who had no recollection of this promise, stood confounded. The bishop had laid much stress upon these words as he uttered them. He continued, solemnly, "Jean Valjean, my brother; you belong no longer to evil, but to good. It is your soul that I am buying for you. I withdraw it from dark thoughts and from the spirit of perdition, and I give it to God!"[2]

The bishop's act of grace had settled all accounts. Jean was released from the bonds of hate. Thereafter, he was transformed into a person of lofty character who had a magnificent capacity for self-sacrifice. All debts on his ledger had been canceled.

Love did heal.

THE MEANS—NOT THE ENDS

The very character and personhood of God helps us to put pain into a new perspective. The way He is tells us something about the role of pain. Suffering is never an ends in itself, but is intended to be a means to a higher and more significant purpose. Affliction is always meant to be transformed by the power of love. Anything and everything can be changed. So when the fiery ordeal is done, gold remains.

The promise of metamorphosis was our starting point in the first chapter. We have considered from many different angles the implications of Paul's conviction that "all things work together for good to them that love the Lord and are called according to His purposes." Put in physical terms, I visualize this promise to be like the process of baking a cake.

Almost every one of the major ingredients in baking is undesirable in its uncooked form. Ever accidentally eat some lard or mistake flour for powdered sugar? Try drinking some vanilla extract or any concentrated artificial flavoring. Even mixed together, cake batter doesn't offer much in the way of personal satisfaction. However, once heat is applied over the right duration, something wonderful occurs and a finished product comes forth.

We call our time in the oven suffering.

Why me? Why not? If I want to be more than "half-baked," I need the heat.

Moreover, suffering is the means by which fear, reluctance, and reservation are transformed until we are able to live with courage. In the end we are enabled to live resolutely and without trepidation. The world is changed, remolded, and redeemed by people who bear in themselves both the weight and the promise of this process.

No one better demonstrated this truth than August Romero. While he did not become a Christian until he was fifty-nine, in a few short years he became the archbishop of the Roman Catholic Church of El Salvador. From this lofty position of authority and responsibility, he surveyed the needs of his country and recognized what had to be done to bring peace and tranquility to his people.

Writing to the president of the United States, he implored Jimmy Carter not to send weapons that would only cause death. He warned that chaos and turmoil would follow military assistance. Even though he clearly argued that U.S. weapons could only make his country more unstable, the archbishop's plea was ignored. Within three years, El Salvador was the third largest recipient of American arms in the Western hemisphere, escalating its instability and political chaos.

On March 23, 1980, five weeks after Archbishop Romero wrote to the United States, he sent a pastoral letter to all the soldiers of El Salvador, imploring them not to obey orders to shoot their own people. Rather, he ordered them in the name of God to stop all killing of their brother and sister citizens. Immediately the Christian generals called the archbishop a traitor and intimated that his days were numbered. Undaunted, the next day Romero made a fearless and unprecedented public announcement of exactly where he would hold mass and what time he would celebrate. His text for the homily was to be his own funeral sermon. He preached to the congregation, "Unless a grain of wheat falls into the earth and dies, it remains alone; but if it dies, it bears much fruit." His words ringing through the great cathedral in San Salvador, proclaiming the opportunity of giving up one's life if necessary, demonstrated his victory in Christ to serve the needs of others. Then he turned to the prayers of consecration. Just as August Romero was about to proclaim the Body of Christ broken for sin, the assassin's shots rang out and he fell to the floor at the foot of the large crucifix. Mortally wounded, the last thing Romero saw was the image of Christ above him.

As he was carried out of the cathedral, his vestment turned crimson, saturated by his blood. Suffering and death had not been imposed, but fearlessly and gladly *chosen* by the archbishop. As the news of his death swept across the country, a wave of mourning and anguish went up to the heavens. His death seemed to be a contradiction of all that he had preached. Defeat and loss settled over the Church of El Salvador.

And yet—and yet. . . . in a few days, a few weeks, a chant began to be heard in the fields and the towns. Growing in crescendo, the slogan swept across the country and resounded through the city streets: "August Romero presente! August Romero presente!" August Romero lives! The grain that fell into the ground bears fruit; the archbishop triumphs from the grave!

In contrast to the national war of political intrigue, something akin to a spiritual revival gripped the country. Unexpected signs of grace began to appear. Generals found it in their hearts to forgive killers and a state of amnesty surfaced. Abused, subjected people almost mystically found a new strength and courage to believe that nothing could stop them on their road to freedom. The life and death of August Romero had become a national symbol that those who are willing to suffer for righteousness' sake will finally be victorious. Through his death, he had accomplished more than in his life.

Never an end, suffering is the means whereby our feeble efforts are multiplied, granting us a portion in the victory that overcomes the world. We, too, are seed and none can predict the harvest of joy.

THE DEPTH DIMENSION

The thorny path to joy was first completely walked by Jesus. He embodied both truth and the potential of transforming love as He faced His own ordeal. Jewish believers living in Rome in the first century were encouraged to follow the model of perseverance totally demonstrated in His cross. They were told to "look to Jesus, the pioneer and perfector of our faith, who for the joy that was set before him endured the cross . . . (Heb. 12:2).

The crucifixion was His means, His *modus operandi*, His route for the recovery of joy. Obviously a methodology of cosmic proportions was at work in that Tree.

As the cross was planted in the Palestinian soil, so it also rooted deeply into human experience. From out of these depths of self-sacrifice arose the joy that made life worth living. Paradoxically, we have to go down to those same taproots where life hurts the most in order to finally reach up to the heights where the most profound joy is to be found. We need not fear times of difficult descent. We must not for a moment lose sight of the promise of the *joie de vivre* to be found from being involved in the alleviation of another's pain. Such was the secret of the courage of August Romero.

In contrast, we live in a society that goes to great lengths to avoid involvement. Discomfort and struggle are viewed as supreme evil. Deprivation and discipline are frustrations to uninhibited self-expression. The slogans of our time are "Look Out for Yourself" and "Keep Your Mouth Shut." The chant in our marketplace is "Not me, it's somebody else's problem." Our age looks at the Cross and tends to respond "That's what you get for sticking your neck out!" We don't like getting out on limbs or going down to the deep.

The ethos of middle class life envisions a climate that is free from all material want. Contact with human suffering is kept at a distance, behind closed doors and out of sight lest we be embarrassed by the personal needs of a dying world. Starving Navajo children, hungry people in America, dying babies in Biafra, street people in large cities, and dispossessed and repossessed farmers are kept from disturbing the facade we cower behind.

Thomas Merton found a new parable to describe the indifference of this age. He viewed the house of Adolph Eichmann in the middle of Auschwitz as an appropriate symbol of our materialism. Surrounded by a huge brick wall, Eichmann's children played with elaborate toys, well-fed and completely oblivious to the millions dying only a few feet away. And so we, too, live in our ghettos of affluence and denial.

Periodically our society erupts in protest against our own moral blindness, denial, and timidity. The artist and the young recognize the hollowness of what we are doing and demand that we face how we have robbed ourselves of the capacity to feel, to care, and to be truly fulfilled. The late sixties witnessed such a time of rebellion against the plastic world that money had created. Songs like "The Sounds of Silence" and "Blowin' in the Wind" protested our emptiness. In turn, that decade's generation of young signed up to give their time to the Peace Corps, knowing that only the recovery of commitment could restore genuine purpose and joy to life.

As the eighties come to a close, a similar disenchantment has arisen. Following a decade of the politics of profit and greed, many youth are sick of our national overdose of self-indulgence. Yuppies and Dinks (double-income, no-kids couples) are out, as well as many other symbols of affluence and indulgence. Once more the meaning of the journey to the Cross makes very practical common sense to the disillusioned who seek joy.

How often have we looked back over the most difficult times in our lives to realize that they were the most fulfilling moments of all? Surveying twenty-three years of ministry, I can see those first days in a very different light now. I had given up a good paying job to be provided with a drafty antique of a house and three thousand dollars a year to take care of my wife and three children. Our rickety old car got so bad that we literally had to tie the back doors together to make sure it was safe for the children. During that particular year we spent one thousand dollars on doctor bills. How did we survive? With great joy. Struggling, crimping, perplexed, and naive, we were living on the cutting edge of where meaning is found. Only in retrospect do we realize how good it was.

Even when we have to force ourselves, joy is found by living beyond our personal preoccupations. No matter how overwhelming our circumstances have been, when we go out to the edges of society to help the disenfranchised, we are granted a new lease on life. To dare to care for people who can never fully say thank you will put us in a place to receive the bestowment of divine pleasure.

OUR INTENTION, HIS WILL?

But we have not exhausted all of the dimensions of why the Pioneer and Perfector of our faith so willingly faced His hour of trial. The Cross depicts another directive for finding true happiness. Jesus saw the Via Dolorosa as God's intention for Himself. Accepting and embracing the will of God always leaves behind the mundane and secure, sending us forth to places where true treasures are buried. While the first phases of the journey may be chaotic and filled with uncertainty, we are traveling on the only road where lasting peace is found.

The quest for the will of God is more than obedience to a divine mandate; it is the final renewal of our own resources for contentment and satisfaction. The decision to relentlessly seek the will of God is one of the most powerful steps for beginning again.

But it's hard for us to know God's will because of our obsession with our own desires. We talk a better story than we live. The obstacles stumbled over along the way often force us to become lucid about our mixed and confused motives. We need opposition to make us look at the many aspects of our own denial and self-deception. Every delusion is a hidden but considerable roadblock in our pursuit of fulfillment. Our lack of clarity only panders to egocentricity, prolongs the recovery of the soul, concealing God's intentions for us.

Dante Alighieri had penetrating insight for us in *The Divine Comedy*. He writes about why we lose sight of both God's best intentions and personal satisfaction. As he traveled through the place of purging, he met three groups of people who had failed to truly fulfill the will of the heavenly Father. As a result, their earthly experiences went uncompleted and their lives unsatisfied.

The first group were not bad people, but they did not really struggle with what God wanted. Avoiding evil, they had little interest in fully embracing the good. While they did not capitulate to the pressures of life, they were not completely faithful to their vows. They compromised.

Next was the company of people of leadership and integrity who fought for good causes. However, their motives were misused with selfishness and vanity. They took too much pride in their own achievements.

The last group had natural gifts of love and were gracious and kind people. Unfortunately, they overindulged themselves, letting their love become sentimental and soft. They were not willing to hold to the hard things that had to be done in the name of love.

From our point of view there is much to be commended in each group. Yet, they all grew weary and fainthearted. They came short in the race set before them. Their failure to struggle fully with the cross set before them robbed them of their joy.

What would have made the difference?

When Dante inquired about their deliverance, he received an extraordinary answer, "*E sua voluntade e nostra pace.*" "His will is our peace." Both the vast ocean in which we all fare as well as the wind that moves us across the waters, His will is also the harbor that we seek. We cannot anchor our lives anywhere else but in completely embracing God's will. Sanctuary awaits our decision to will only one will. His will and our peace are one thing. Beyond knowing, beyond doing, serenity is found only in fully wanting what He wants.

Such singleness of vision and mind can't be found without a personal emptying of ego that isn't possible without considerable pain. It is accessible only when the designs and manipulations of the ego are pushed aside in order that unity with God's will can settle into the soul. One of the great assets of our brokenness is that it brings us to the place of total self-surrender as nothing else can. Once we have gotten past anger and are simply abiding in the place of our hurt, we are at the threshold of that awesome inner chapel when we can truly and fully pray, "Nothing in heaven and earth do I desire but Thee, O Lord." These moments of consecration are the most profitable times in our lives.

Nothing demonstrates this principle as does the agony and cruelty of the Cross, which was the ultimate means by which Jesus demonstrated the joy of embracing the Father's will. Our traveling companion, Paul, again paints the picture for us:

Have this mind in you which you have in Christ

Jesus, who, though he was in the form of God, did
not count equality with God a thing to be grasped,
but emptied himself, taking the form of a servant,
being born in the likeness of men. And being found in
human form he humbled himself and became obedient
unto death, even death on a cross. Therefore, God has
highly exalted him and bestowed on him the name
which is above every name.[3]

Sooner or later we all find ourselves on a cross of some
variety. The critical issue will be our ability to pray,
"Father, forgive, for they know not." The very act of embracing His will at that moment is the first step toward
serenity.

For the joy set before Him, Christ Jesus pursued the
will of the Father without variance. Praying "Not my
will but thine be done" in the Garden of Gethsemane,
Jesus was staring the final despair in the face. Without
blinking He saw the cost. But seeing beyond, He also
comprehended the final satisfaction found by all who set
themselves aside. Our full recovery of joy requires a
similar response.

AND DOES IT WORK?

The *Imago Dei* and the soul are source and reflection.
Objectively, we have been created in the image of God.
The subjective expression of that fact is my soul. When I
am a mirror of my Creator, my life is filled with joy. More
than mere happiness, I am promised an inner subterra-
nean flow of sustaining satisfaction that imparts well-
being in both good and bad times. The preceding
paragraphs have suggested where the headwaters of
this joy are found.

First, I must live beyond the desire for vindication and
retribution. Life basically isn't fair and most tragic situations never can be justified or validated by any explanation. Stop trying to balance the books.

Second, regardless of what happens, I will respond in
love. I can't control anyone else's actions, but I am re-

sponsible for my reactions. Love is the only path to joy.

Third, if the defenselessness of God is His superiority, then surely I can quit being so defensive. I have to give up some of my turf if I am going to gain any ground in this battle with pain. The degree to which I am vulnerable will be the measure of the joy I receive.

Fourth, I must want the will of God more than anything else. Joy is found on the other side of "letting go." His will is our peace.

But here's the *big* question. Do these ideas, convictions, and beliefs work? Will these principles really lead me to a full recovery of joy? Well, here's my experience.

In the earlier chapters I touched on some aspects of my own journey through pain. At every point where I was stripped of some facet of my past experience, I found that with the loss came an unexpected gain. What I wouldn't have chosen to give up finally became new opportunity. Perhaps the most unexpected discovery was my own reconciliation with myself. So much of what I was wasn't acceptable to me. I couldn't face the truth about feelings of inadequacy, low self-esteem, and basic fears for survival. As long as I kept the negative emotions downstairs, they soured and festered. Once they were embraced, the pain became gain. I remember vividly the day I first realized that something had changed inside.

I was in a heated argument boring in on my opponent like a trial lawyer before the Supreme Court. The other side was coming back with increasingly heated salvos of anger. Our voices were escalating in pitch and intensity. Suddenly something in my head said, "You don't have to win this conversation. Nothing is this important."

Although the other side hadn't missed a beat, I began to lower my voice. Finally I said quietly, "Perhaps you're right."

"What?" she said with a look of surprise. "What do you mean?"

"Maybe there's something more useful here than one of us prevailing."

As the tenor of the whole confrontation changed, I was aware of a deep sense of satisfaction that I hadn't often known. Earlier I had come to see that my childhood abuse had created an inordinate desire for justice. I had to fight so hard because the little child inside of me was terrified of being victimized. But the stripping process had shown me that the best we ever get is forgiveness, and most of the time we're the ones who have to pass it out. So I didn't have to win every time. Yes, living beyond justice and trying to express love worked.

Getting things right within me made it much easier to take care of what had gone wrong on the outside. I found that my memory kept coughing up unfinished business in relationships that had gone sour. I knew joy was on hold until I went back and untangled those knotted ends. One such conversation came at Christmas time.

During a building project I had become deeply angered with a man I felt had not served us well. Bitterness grew up between us. Our final financial transactions had become so muddled that we could have ended up in a lawsuit. Christmas was approaching, and as I prepared to celebrate the joy of the birth of the Christ Child, I began to realize that our confrontations had affected this man's self-worth. How could I be filled with the Christmas spirit while I had diminished another human being's ability to be happy? So I called him up, took him out for coffee, and we reconciled. When we shook hands, I wished him a merry Christmas. As I turned toward my car, I was immediately filled with a joy beyond anything I had previously known. He had given the gift of forgiveness.

The amazing thing about our fears is that they thrive in darkness and dissolve in light. Once we are able to touch them, they tend to shrivel, shrink, and disappear. I found that I was able to restore many broken relationships when I put my fears of rejection aside. I want to encourage you, in your struggle, to do the same. There are few experiences as meaningful and satisfying as reconciliation.

Still, there is one necessary step beyond what I have already described. The recovery of the soul allows one to live beyond egocentricity; we must escape our preoccupation with protecting the self. In such moments we are able to touch the joy of life itself. In those times the wonder of life is so rich that we become truly thankful for whatever pain was necessary to open our eyes and unstop our ears.

I discovered that Mr. Ego had always made me a detached observer and distant participant. His posture had caused me to stand back and muse whether it was safe to really get involved. However, when my soul was at the point of contact, I was able to enter in and know the full richness and wonder of what I was experiencing. I found that I looked at pictures and heard music in a different way. Colors and sounds wrapped themselves around my imagination and thrilled me with their brilliance and poignancy. When I talked with people, I would become aware of their essence like smelling a luxurious perfume. No matter what they looked like physically or the extent of their limitations, I found something special about them that gave me a glimpse of the image of God. Handicapped, retarded, deformed—all come with their own beauty.

Worship became richer than it had ever been. In the past my inner spiritual conversations had run something like this, "It's time for 'us' to talk to God. 'I' will praise God. Let 'me' sing a stirring song to get in the mood for spiritual things." Lots of ego in all of those admonitions.

In contrast, I found that my soul could reach up beyond restraints or controls that I had previously tried to exercise—to touch what no eye could ever see. The Holy Spirit's presence was free to move as He chose, not as I manipulated. A new closeness was achieved that was beyond anything I could have created. Regardless of how much difficulty or pain seemed to be swirling around me, the reality of God quickly became the most certain factor in my life. I had found the meaning of Paul's declaration that he knew how to both abound and be abased,

the secret of having everything and having nothing.
Only the soul can fully comprehend how, in everything,
God is working for the good for those who love Him.
Therein is supreme joy.

DINING ALONE

Following the will of God is never an invitation to constant entertainment. There are inevitable moments in
the journey when we must travel alone. And loneliness
isn't easy.

The apostle John gives us an intriguing vignette from
the life of Jesus in which John addresses the need for
isolation. Concerned about whether Jesus had been
served lunch, the disciples said rather forcefully, "Rabbi,
eat!"

Jesus responded to the effect, "I've been chewing on
something by myself of which you know nothing."

To try to lift their minds higher than their stomachs so
they might have a more lofty vision of their purpose in
life, Jesus answered, "My food is to do the will of Him
who sent me, and to accomplish His work."[4] Life is more
than comfort and physical satisfaction. Without solitude,
the task couldn't be accomplished.

To be nourished on the provisions of heaven requires
lots of dining alone. Even the hint of such complete isolation can send some people frantically searching for
anyone or anything to fill the vacuum with sounds
reassuring them they haven't been left. Yet, there is an
abandonment that we must face if we are to find the joy
of being fully satisfied by having been fed from the hand
of God.

I first realized the poignancy of this fact a number of
years ago when I was listening to a rendition of George
Bernard Shaw's *Saint Joan*. The French were embroiled
in battle and Joan was urging the king on in the fight.
Surrounded by complacent advisors, he is told to stop. If
they follow Joan of Arc one more time, their luck may
run out and disaster will follow. The aides warn that vic-

tories won by this strange woman have only been coincidental.

Joan protests that luck never had anything to do with her success. God was on her side because their cause was just. The aides chide her that if she tries it again and fails, she will be alone. Neither army nor church nor king could save her in such a defeat. She will be utterly alone.

Instantly she answers, "Loneliness is the strength of God! Because God is alone, God is strong. When I am alone, I am strongest."

Joan had discovered that armed only with her integrity, she was prepared. When she didn't have to wait for any institution, army, or man, she had come to the place where no one could stop the charge. At such a lonely moment, she was in touch with the greatest strength in the world. Her food was to do the will of Him who sent her.

I find it easy to make talks about such times, but hard to saddle up and charge into them. Yet, only by standing alone am I finally unafraid. The only insurance we have against being dehumanized by our struggles comes from remaining true to ourselves in these moments of isolation. Out of the silence the soul emerges. Loneliness is the strength of God, so He feeds us from His plate.

In loneliness we find what T. S. Eliot called "the still point of the turning world."

CONCLUSIONS

In coldest days of winter when snow is deepest, it is hard to believe that beneath the ice the promise of summer waits. Yet as days lengthen and nights shorten, so in the seasons of life spring comes again. We are meant to be like hidden seed, waiting for the warmth of better days. Alone and concealed, if we draw all that is around us to ourselves, like grain preparing for germination, new life will break forth. In due time we shall fulfill our promise.

How shall we recover our joy? Here are principles of planting awaiting our practice.

- His will is our peace.
  The quest for singleness of mind, heart, and
  soul is the starting point. We must bury our-
  selves in the purpose of the heavenly Father.
- All suffering is meant to be transformed.
  Trust the process to end in joy. The time in
  darkness will end in light.
- Love alone heals.
  Responding lovingly restores, reconciles, and
  recovers joy.
- Forget justice; find forgiveness.
  The world isn't fair. But if we work to make it
  so for others, it will become so for us.
- When you are alone, you are never alone.
  We must get by ourselves to reach the place
  where we can really be with God. Solitude
  is where we receive the strength and joy of
  God.

All things will work together. Growing into the image
of Christ contains the promise of a fullness that draws
joy from the abundance of life which He brought. The
future is never confined or limited to what I can see.
Undaunted, the Light of the world always makes all
nights temporary. Even when I don't see it, can't remember it, or hope for it, the dawn is yet to be.

As the psalmist wrote, "He has kept my tears in his
bottle," making full notation of my tossings and turn-
ings. In due time there shall be an accounting when the
day breaks, revealing that which has been hidden. In
that hour, I will rejoice at what shall come forth.

What will I see? Nothing less than my own soul per-
fected by pain. The veneer of artificiality and delusion
will be peeled away. Hidden places of fear, guilt, anger,
and shame will be cleansed and healed. Brokenness and
woundedness will be changed from scars to wrinkles
and lines of wisdom that are found only on the faces of
seasoned sages. The recovery of such a soul is worth any
cost. There is joy promised to the people of God.

We shall prevail.

". . . the night is far gone,
  the day is at hand.
Let us then cast off the works of darkness
  and put on the armor of light" (Rom. 13:12).

Notes

Chapter 1 Has God Abandoned Me or Did I Abandon Him?

1. Romans 8:28.
2. Ernest Hemingway, "Tragedy of an Evangelical," *Christianity Today,* 28 November 1984, 20.
3. Ibid, 27.

Chapter 2 What Are the Enemies of My Soul?

1. Poem written by Ruth Harms Calkin, "Once and for All." Used by permission.

Chapter 3 What Good Is There in So Much Bad?

1. Romans 8:28.
2. Romans 8:29.
3. 1 Peter 2:21
4. Romans 8:18-19.

Chapter 4 Can I Come Through Pain to Personhood?

1. Joel Fort, *The Addicted Society* (New York: Grove Press, Inc., 1981), 31-32.
2. Benjamin Spock, "How Onscreen Violence Hurts Your Kids," *Redbook*, November 1987, 26.
3. Kate Moody, *Growing Up on Television* (New York: TIMES Books, 1980), 82.
4. Peggy Charren and Martin W. Sandler, *Changing Channels* (Reading, Mass.: Addison Wesley Publishing Co., 1983), 171.
5. Quoted in Robert Raines, *Creative Brooding* (New York: Macmillan Co., 1966), 79.

Chapter 5 Where Is My Center and My Circumference?

1. Chaim Potok, *The Chosen* (Greenwich, Conn.: Fawcett Publications, 1965), 265.
2. Gerhard Kittel, *Theological Dictionary of the New Testament*, vol. 9 (Grand Rapids: Eerdman's, 1974), 608-617.
3. Ibid, 627.
4. Proverbs 4:21-23.
5. Deuteronomy 10:16, 30:6; Psalm 51:10-13; Ezekiel 11:19-21, 36:26-27.
6. Jeremiah 17:9; Zechariah 7:12.
7. Exodus 6:9; Hosea 4:12; Numbers 5:14; 1 Chronicles 5:26; 2 Chronicles 12:4-13.
8. John 16:12-15; Acts 2:14-21; Romans 8:5-11; 1 Corinthians 12:4-13.

9. Haggai 1:14.
10. Gerhard Kittel, *op. cit.*, 642–649.
11. Ecclesiastes 3:11, 12:5.
12. 3 John 2.
13. Carl G. Jung, *Modern Man in Search of a Soul* (Harcourt, Brace, Jovanovich, 1933), 221–244.

Chapter 6 Can I Recover My Soul?

1. Luke 9:23–25.
2. Galatians 2:20.

Chapter 7 Am I Being Tested, Tempted, or Tried?

1. 1 Corinthians 10:13.
2. Romans 5:3–4.

Chapter 8 Is My Soul Wounded?

1. Isaiah 43:18–19.
2. Robert L. Wise, *Healing the Past* (Oklahoma City: Presbyterian and Reformed Renewal Ministries, 1984). This story and others with an expanded explanation of inner healing are included in this booklet.
3. Matthew 5:44.
4. John 8:7.

Chapter 9 Is the Night Endless?

1. Romans 8:35–39.
2. 1 John 5:11–14.
3. Norman Vincent Peale, *The True Joy of Positive Living* (Pauling, New York: Foundation for Christian Living, 1984), 283–288.

Chapter 10 Can I Face the Emptiness?

1. John 14:16–18.
2. 2 Corinthians 1:3–4.
3. 2 Corinthians 1:5.
4. Galatians 2:20.

Chapter 11 Can I Recover My Joy?

1. 1 Peter 2:21–24.
2. Victor Hugo, *Les Miserables* (New York: Dodd, Mead and Company), 27–28.
3. Philippians 2:5–9.
4. John 4:31–34.